The Int

an

World Wide Web

explained

Other Titles of Interest

The Internet
and
World Wide Web
explained

by

John Shelley

BERNARD BABANI (publishing) LTD
THE GRAMPIANS
SHEPHERDS BUSH ROAD
LONDON W6 7NF
ENGLAND

PLEASE NOTE

Although every care has been taken with the production of this book to ensure that any projects, designs, modifications and/or programs, etc., contained herewith, operate in a correct and safe manner and also that any components specified are normally available in Great Britain, the Publishers and Author(s) do not accept responsibility in any way for the failure (including fault in design) of any project, design, modification or program to work correctly or to cause damage to any equipment that it may be connected to or used in conjucntion with, or in respect of any other damage or injury that may be so caused, nor do the Publishers accept responsibility in any way for the failure to obtain specified components.

Notice is also given that if equipment that is still under warranty is modified in any way or used or connected with home-built equipment then that warranty may be void.

© 1996 BERNARD BABANI (publishing) LTD

First Published - January 1996
Reprinted - September 1996

British Library Cataloguing in Publication Data

A catalogue record for this book is available from the British Library

ISBN 0 85934 403 7

Printed and Bound in Great Britain by Cox & Wyman Ltd, Reading

About this Book

This text explains what the Information Superhighway is all about, how my computer, the Internet and the World Wide Web interconnect and how they work. It also answers many questions such as:

- what is the Information Superhighway?
- what use is it to me?
- how does it work?
- where is it going?
- can I connect my home or office PC to the Internet?
- can I really get sound and movies as well as text?
- what do I need to access the Information Superhighway?
- how much will it cost?
- who controls the Highway?
- will I be 'attacked' by hackers and viruses?
- can my e-mail messages be read by the whole world?
- will I be able to discuss my particular interests with others of a like mind all around the world?

Who needs to Know?

There are 4 levels, at least:

- those who have a general interest or curiosity about the Internet
- those who wish to use it - for example, to find information or send and receive e-mail
- those who need or would like to put information onto the Information Superhighway as well as use it

- those who have more sophisticated uses, such as those responsible for their local network

This book caters for the first three levels explaining in simple English many of the jargon terms we all meet when using the Information Superhighway. Those in the second and third categories may require, in addition to the basic introduction provided here, some training in the use of their local system. Sorry but that's life! The fourth group will know where to find their own in-depth training.

Despite all the media hype and an assumption that the Internet is only for those with four pairs of spectacles and a wardrobe full of anoraks the vast majority of users are quite ordinary and staid. They are simply trying to come to terms with and benefit from this latest technology.

The Information Superhighway is not just for large academic and business organisations. Smaller companies, charities and societies, as well as many individuals will benefit from what it has to offer.

Ten years ago, many people were mildly interested in something called *microcomputers*. Now look where we all are. The same may be true of the Information Superhighway; who will not be using it in five or ten years time?

About the Author

John Shelley took his Masters degree in Computing at Imperial College, London, where he has worked as a lecturer in the Centre for Computing Services for some twenty-five years.

He has been Chief Examiner since 1982 for the Oxford Local Delegacy in Computer Studies for their GCE O-level examinations, Senior Examiner for the SEG GCSE Computer Studies (now both defunct) and, at the time of writing, Chief Examiner for O-level Computer Studies for Overseas candidates. Yes! such an examination still exists beyond these shores.

He has written nine other books on computing. This is his latest text which he hopes will prove useful to those who want to learn about the Internet at a human level.

He is married with one daughter. We would like to dedicate this book to:

SAM & PEPE

Trademarks

Microsoft, MS-DOS, Microsoft Windows, Windows 3.1, Windows 95, Internet Assistant are registered trademarks of Microsoft Corporation.

IBM, Token Ring, are registered trademarks of International Business Machines Corporation.

Ethernet is a registered trademark of Digital Equipment Corporation, Intel and Xerox Corporation.

Unix is a registered trademark of AT&T.

WordPerfect, Ami-Pro, Word 6, Eudora, Netscape, Mosaic, Cello, SLIP, PPP, Kermit, PROCOMM, Demon, Ping, SURFNET, EUnet, CU-SeeMe, Doctor Fun, Amiga, Archimedes, Atari are registered trademarks or copyrights of their relevant organisations.

Mac, Apple Macintosh, PowerMac, Sun, Intel, Mercury, BT, Energis, are registered trademarks or copyrights of their relevant organisations.

IEEE, SunSite, Delphi, Clarinet are registered trademarks or copyrights of their relevant organisations.

References to the various URLs on the Internet are acknowledged here.

All other trademarks are the registered and legally protected trademarks of the companies who make the products. There is no intent to use the trademarks generically and readers should investigate ownership of a trademark before using it for any purpose.

Contents

Part A - Introduction

Part B - How it is all put together

Chapter 7: The World Wide Web

Chapter 8: Earlier Internet Tools

Chapter 9: How to Put Information on to the Highway

Part C - Social and Practical Issues

Chapter 10: What Do I Need to Connect to the Internet and the WWW?

Chapter 11: Security: Hackers and Viruses

Part A - Introduction

Chapter 1: The Information Superhighway

The Information Superhighway, the Internet and the World Wide Web

What is their connection?

Information is currently held in many computer sites situated all over the world. As an example, the University of Michigan (USA) provides information about weather conditions[1] for the entire United States. I could contact this source of information from my home computer in Watford, England, to find out about the weather in Fort Wayne, Indiana where my sister lives. The latest phrase for accessing this world wide depository of information is the *Information Superhighway* or, sometimes, *Cyberspace*.

The mechanism whereby my home computer becomes linked to the Michigan computer site is the *Internet*. The means by which I can display on my computer screen the details of the weather stored on the University of Michigan's computer system is the *World Wide Web*. We shall explain all three in detail.

The Information Superhighway

At a simple level, the Information Superhighway is merely a collection of information[2] which anyone can

---

[1] It is stored on a database called the *Weather Underground*.
[2] It is getting richer all the time - not only text but images, movies, sound and the ability to fill in and send off forms to register for courses, order goods, obtain new computer games, etc.

tap into. It is also a source which anyone can add to, even you and me. For example, I could put on my own photograph and a potted life history of myself, so that anyone anywhere in the world could see what I look like and learn something about me. I could even sing a song for the whole world to hear. To do so would be expensive (see Chapter 10 for costing). Chapter 9 discusses how one goes about putting information onto the Highway.

It is the *Internet* which allows the physical access to the information on the Highway. Everyone linked to the Internet ("on the Net") can access the information on the Information Superhighway, including my potted life history.

What Type of Information goes on the Highway?

In theory, almost anything. The information put on is that which might be of interest to other people. If you think that some piece of information or knowledge or your own personal opinion might be of interest to someone, somewhere out there, put it on the Information Superhighway. It could be a new type of rose that you have created, details about cakes which you bake and how to order them, a profile of your company, or some rare insect discovered in a South American forest. Since sound and images can also be added along with ordinary text, then pictures and real sounds of the insect (or your music group) can be made available.

This, of course, is so general that almost anything could go on the Highway. Chapter 4 discusses how information is "monitored" before being allowed on.

What Type of Information can I get?

Whatever is available! Some of it is bizarre, some highly informative, some relates to special interest groups, for example, music, biology, computer science, new software, bridge, chess, sport, art. You can also join in world-wide discussion groups, ask questions, reply to questions and 'meet' new friends.

There is a story (there are many around and I cannot guarantee this one's authenticity) about someone in the States having a technical problem trying to install some equipment. Being alone, he could not get advice so he asked his question over the Internet to the entire world. A little while later he was amazed to get a reply from someone in Australia explaining how to do it.

More information is being put on the Information Superhighway by the day and by the hour. If you read the history section, Chapter 3, you will see that the Internet was developed originally out of a desire for research and education. Consequently, what has already been put up on the Information Superhighway is very much of that nature. However, as more and more people, particularly from commerce and industry, are realising the capability of the Highway, much more diverse information is becoming available. Not only can you find beer recipes, 25 years of recorded Hard Rock and Heavy Metal, science fiction, and a daily cartoon, but also recent Supreme Court rulings, warnings about the latest viruses, company products and profiles, and, unhappily, pornography, anarchy, etc.

To give a flavour of some of the more healthy topics which can be tapped into, here are a few, some of their contact addresses are given in Appendix A:

- Many universities provide details about their courses, staff, campus facilities, etc., even some test examination papers.

- The most recent upgrades to operating systems, computer hardware, computer games, etc.

- Many companies, particularly those who provide Internet services, give details about their products and even allow their goods to be ordered over the Internet.

- A special project, HERMES, make the US Supreme Court's opinions and rulings available.

- Museums, art galleries, libraries, etc., supply not only details of openings times and costs, but some include pictures of their exhibits; for example, images of illustrated manuscripts held at the Bodleian Library.

- Some government departments, for example, the CIA and NASA, provide certain information about their organisations.

- There is an indexed film database with synopses, cast lists, etc., for over 6500 films.

- But there is much, much more. If you want cooking recipes, lists of published books, assistance in planning and planting a garden, a history of the tango, it is all there on the Information Superhighway.

- You may be a teenager who cannot talk to your parents about French medieval poetry and no one in town seems to care much either. Then you could start up a 'discussion' group over the

Highway, if one does not already exist, and reach out to the entire world to find others of a like mind, rather like radio hams, indeed, there is a Radio Ham hobby group.

- There are news groups, sometimes called Bulletin Board systems, whereby people exchange information about a whole host of topics. If you have a hobby you can exchange information with people of a similar persuasion.

- Before too long, you may even be able to sing on the Highway. If you have a multi-media computer with a sound card and CD-Rom you will be able to download songs, store them on your machine and listen to them whilst you do your word processing.

- It is not just a place to find information, it is also a valuable tool for commerce. You can check exchange rates, share prices and other business news. You can contact business colleagues all around the world, and more effectively than relying on answer-phones.

Who pays for all this and who controls what goes on is discussed below but, first, how does it work?

Chapter 2: How Does it Work?

The Internet allows one person via their own computer to contact someone else's computer anywhere in the world. The two people do not have to have the same type of computer and probably will not. They could have an IBM PC, a Mac, Amiga, Archimedes, Atari, a Unix workstation[3] or a large mainframe. The Internet is an international network comprising many different types of computers. To make contact, each person requires:

- a computer which is linked to an Internet network (via a modem in their own home or by a direct line[4] from their office)
- software which can send information over the Internet as well as receive information and display it on a screen

Networks have existed for several decades, so what made the Internet so special? Simply, it is difficult to *destroy*. This makes more sense once we understand how networks operate. It is now time to look more closely at what is a basic network. We shall, then, be in a position to appreciate the Internet itself and see just where the Information Superhighway fits in to the Internet.

---

[3] These are larger and more powerful than PCs or Macs and are often used to control the transmission of electronic mail messages between our smaller computers.
[4] A direct line can carry data for about 150 metres, but this can be extended by use of amplifiers & repeaters, and there is no need for a modem. See Chapter 10 for more details.

What is a network?

The original concept of a network came about for several reasons, one being that a person at one computer wanted to send information (a message) to someone else at another computer. To do so, both computers had to be connected together, i.e. networked. Let us assume a building with ten micro computers scattered around in various offices. If they could be linked together, then they could send messages to each other rather than having to rely on their internal mail system.

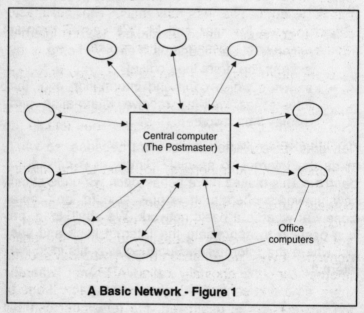

A Basic Network - Figure 1

For one machine to send a message to another machine, something has to organise and control the whole operation. (See Figure 1.) This is an eleventh computer complete with specially written programs which can receive messages from any one of the ten machines and redirect them to the correct person (machine). This is what the postmaster does at a local post office, indeed, this special computer is frequently referred to as a *postmaster*. It is more efficient to have one machine dedicated to this task rather than all ten linked to each other.

If I wish to send a message to Ms X, I would use the software on my machine, say an electronic mail (e-mail) program, to compose (type) the message and to send it to the postmaster. When Ms X switches on her machine, she would use her e-mail program (which could be different to mine) to contact the postmaster to check whether she has any mail. The postmaster would forward the mail and Ms X's e-mail program would display my message on her screen.

Now the point is this. If I wanted to destroy the entire set-up, all I would need to do is to destroy one machine, the eleventh one, the postmaster, the central one. Then the other ten would be unable to communicate with each other any more.

Communication is important, not least to the military, particularly in time of war. They need to keep in contact through one of many different means and one such method is via a computer network. However, if the central postmaster is destroyed, so is the entire network. It was the American military who devised the Internet concept, originally called ARPAnet, whereby there is no *one* centralised system but *many*. If one of the postmasters is destroyed, the remainder can still function. (See Figure 2. Put your finger over any one of the centres and you will see that the others can still function.)

Incidentally, it was the demands of World War II which had a direct bearing on the development of the computer itself. Initially, to decode enemy codes and to work out accurately the optimum firing range of big guns.

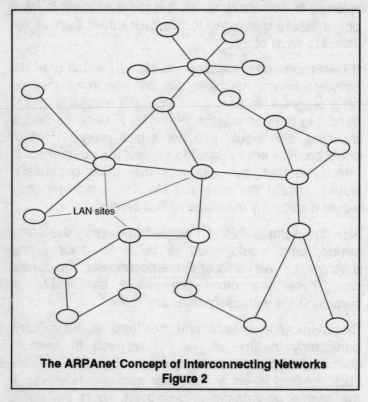

LAN sites

The ARPAnet Concept of Interconnecting Networks
Figure 2

Networks were developed not only to send e-mail but also to share scarce resources such as high quality printers, scanners, as well as shared data bases and programs. Four basic categories of networks[5] grew up: local area networks (LANs) for use in a restricted area such as a building; wide area networks (WANs) linking computers scattered over a town, country or

[5] See *An Introduction to Networks for PC and Mac Users* by D, C & O Bishop, published by Bernard Babani, for more detail about networks.

continents; bulletin board systems (BBS) whereby people 'posted' information for others to read; and, the Internet.

It was the Internet which made the Information Superhighway possible. We next discuss how the Internet came about.

Chapter 3: How the Internet Came About

The ARPAnet

The Internet was conceived in 1969 by the American Defence Department when the Cold War and the Vietnam War were causing civil unrest. It was an experiment in how to design a network which could still function even if one part were to be destroyed by, say, a bomb attack, terrorist activity, an earthquake or simply someone cutting through a cable. It was called the ARPAnet.[6]

A working model was created and academics and researchers were also allowed access. They soon became addicted. Elsewhere in the States, Scandinavia and the UK, demands for similar networks began to grow.

Around the same time, Ethernet local area networks (LANs) were being developed. It was a gradual process until about 1983 when desktop workstations became available and, then, local networking really exploded[7]. Some of the local networks wanted to link up to the ARPAnet to access facilities previously available only to a limited number of researchers and academics.

---

[6] Advanced Research Project Agency. They had four sites in 1969, 4000 by 1983. At one period its name became DARPAnet, the D standing for Defence.

[7] One example was the Joint Academic Network (JANET) established to link many of the major universities in the UK. Later, faster lines were put in and it became SUPERJANET.

13

National Science Foundation

Private networks were also being developed during this period by companies and other organisations. One of the most important of these was the NSFNET system commissioned by the National Science Foundation, an agency of the American government.

In the late 1980s, it created supercomputer centres at renowned American universities. Because of the vast expense of each centre only five were created. The intention was to make the resources at these centres available for scholarly research elsewhere. The problem was how?

NSF approached ARPAnet to use their system. This ploy failed mainly because of bureaucratic and staffing problems. So, NSF decided to build their own network but based on the ARPAnet technology. The five sites were inter-connected by telephone lines able to transmit two A4 pages of data per second (56,000 bits[8] per second, slow by today's standards). But what about the other outlying centres, how were they to join up? Clearly direct lines from each outstation anywhere in the States to one of the five Centres would become prohibitively expensive.

The solution was to create regional network centres, with each one linking up to the next to form a chain. Each chain was eventually linked to one of the five main sites, collectively referred to as the *backbone*. Since each of the five sites were connected, one computer in any one of the chained links could communicate with another computer in any of the other

---

[8] Short for **B**inary dig**IT**, 0 & 1, the system used to store information in computers.

chains as well as with any one of the five main centres. See Figure 3.

It worked, and suddenly regional centres had access to all the data and research available anywhere in the network as well as the use of the special computing facilities at any of the five supercomputer sites. But it worked too well and became overloaded. In 1987, Merit Network Inc. was given a contract to manage and upgrade the network. Faster telephone lines and faster computers were installed and this process of upgrading has had to continue to the present day and must do so into the future.

So successful was the work resulting from the NSF project that it funded connections for other centres but only on the condition that they allowed yet others to connect to them. The Internet had arrived! Not just as a single network but as a network of networks, with more joining in every month.

It was not long before other universities, libraries and research centres in major corporations wanted to join in and not only from the US but also from abroad. Today, of course, it is not restricted to research and education. Neither is access restricted solely from the office computer. Many want to continue their work from their home computers.

To illustrate the cost-effectiveness of the Internet, a colleague of mine was doing research in a particular field which demanded the use of a very powerful supercomputer. He had to connect to a university in the States which had such a computer. Some of his work had to be carried out from his home via a modem and telephone link to the States. Each dial-in session was, of course, expensive. It was a direct call to the States after all. Then the Internet arrived. By connecting to a local Internet network he had the same access to the States computer as before but at the cost of a local telephone call.

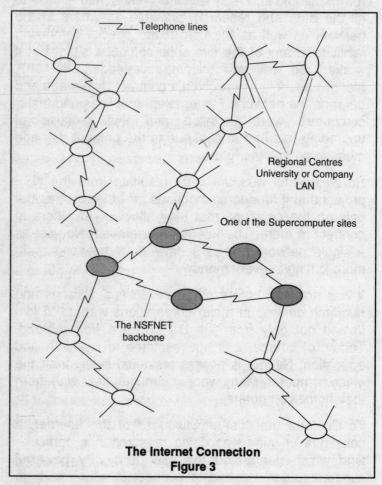

Telephone lines

Regional Centres
University or Company
LAN

One of the Supercomputer sites

The NSFNET
backbone

The Internet Connection
Figure 3

A Common Language

It was not purely the existence of many networks that brought about the Internet. Of far greater significance was how they all managed to 'talk' to each other. The reality of the Internet is a mass of different computers using a variety of operating systems which cannot communicate with (talk to) each other. For example, basic PCs, Macs, Unix workstations, IBM mainframes, Suns, etc., a real Tower of Babel. Some common tongue was required so that all these different computer systems could understand each other. This was another major achievement of the ARPAnet, perhaps the real accomplishment.

The ARPAnet system devised rules (or *protocols* as they are known) for transmitting data, the so-called, Internet Protocol (IP). This is discussed in more detail in Part B.

As the growth in networks increased, so the computers attached to them became many and diverse. If these different systems wanted to communicate with each other, a common language had to be devised. One already existed and worked, the IP protocol; ergo, use that one. It was fortunate that many of the network systems decided to adopt the same IP protocol which ARPAnet had developed, mainly for purely practical reasons.

With the desktop workstation explosion in the mid-80s many of these came with the Berkeley Unix operating system which, fortunately, had also adopted the IP networking protocol. It was this common tongue that led to the world-wide development of the Internet.

NSFNET, although denied use of the ARPAnet's communications, nevertheless based their network strategy on the IP technology. In other words, all those networks mushrooming up all over the place already had a common tongue and were able to link together with comparative ease because they could all talk the same language no matter what operating system or hardware manufacturer they used.

Chapter 4: Who Controls the Internet?

Who Pays for It?

No one and everyone. There is no one body or organisation. There is no one leader. Each computer network is an equal or, in the jargon, a *peer*. Individual institutions pay for their own network which forms a part of the overall Internet. NSF pays for the NSFNET;[9] NASA pays for its Science Internet; Imperial College, London, pays for its connection, and so on. Each corporation or educational centre pays for its connection to a regional centre network. Each regional centre pays for its connection to a national centre, usually a telephone company. Smaller companies, societies and home computer users will pay monthly fees for their access to some commercial provider (often called a *service provider*) which in turn pays for its connection to some other larger provider.

If one of these can no longer pay, then it is no longer a part of the Internet.

Who Controls the Internet?

Again, there is no single body. However, there is an Internet Society, ISOC, a voluntary body whose main purpose is to promote universal exchange of information via the Internet. ISOC appoints members to the IAB (Internet Architecture Board) who in turn decide issues affecting the technical management and overall direction of the Internet. One of the main areas of its remit is to create or maintain standard methods

---

[9] On 30th April 1995, NSFNET was turned off for good. See Chapter 13 for more details.

for different computers to communicate with each other. It meets on a regular basis.

Anyone who has an opinion about how the Internet functions or should function can express their views through another body which holds regular meetings. This is the IETF, the Internet Engineering Task Force. It is another voluntary body but has no real executive power. If its members become concerned about a particular matter, it can make representation to the IAB or to the users of the Internet world in general. Either can adopt or reject the proposal, for example, an agreement on some standard form of documentation.

There are several other bodies, such as the Electronic Frontier Foundation (EFF) founded in 1990. It is concerned, amongst other matters, about social and policy issues mainly on behalf of Internet users.

Apart from these formal bodies, it is the individual network centres which tend to control who and what is allowed on to their network. A university centre may have to restrict the type of organisation allowed to access the Internet through its network to that of a research and educational nature. A commercial company allowing all and sundry within its local vicinity to access (at a fee) the Internet may not be so restrictive. However, it would always hold the right to disconnect an individual should that individual breach common decency or whatever. However, this is not a simple matter and Chapter 12 discusses some of the legal, political and moral issues involved.

It is now time to get down to some technical details, to see how the Internet actually works. It is not everyone who wants to know how things work, but should you take the time, it will explain many of the strange things which appear, such as the four figure numerical addresses. It will also clarify much of the jargon, such as domain names, IP address, hosts, client-servers, hypertext. This will all help to understand what the network gurus are trying to say to you when you ask them simple questions.

E-Mail Abbreviations

If you join in discussion groups, here are a few of the many abbreviations which you may come across.

AFAIK	as far as I know
BFN	bye for now
BTW	by the way
FAQ	frequently asked questions
FWIW	for what it's worth
FYI	for your information
IMCO	in my considered opinion
IMHO	in my humble opinion
OIC	Oh, I see!
OTOH	on the other hand
ROFL	rolls on floor laughing
RTFM	read the friendly manual

Video Conferencing

There are some audio and visual applications being used on the Net. As yet they are not practical for the average home user. The most powerful system is the Multicast Backbone (MBone) but is restricted to centres with fast, high-powered workstations.

For those without such access, Cornell University in Ithaca, New York, has developed a version called CU-SeeMe. It can be used on PCs and Macs provided you have video cards and cameras and a fast direct link to the Internet. It allows people to participate in interactive video conferences. In time, this system may become more generally available and at a price the average home user can afford.

Part B - How it is all put together

In this part, you will meet many of the jargon terms which occur throughout the Information Superhighway, such as *ftp, http://, gopher, TCP/IP, domain names, URL*. They are explained in simple English. You will need to understand them if you wish to explore what is on the Highway or to join in discussion groups.

Chapter 5: How the Internet Works

In order to understand how the Internet works we do need to appreciate some technical terms, otherwise it will always remain 'a bit of a mystery'. Furthermore, knowing something about how the Internet works and where it came from will help to understand the culture of the Net and its spirit of co-operation.

At the basic level, a wire from my computer links it to my local area network (LAN). The wire to my LAN could be a direct wire of a fixed length or a modem connection via the telephone system. My network has other wires linking it to yet more networks which have wires to yet other networks. It is my local network which provides the link between my computer and the Internet. See Figure 4.

Most of the Internet is made up of the telephone system[10] which links one network to another and across continents. However, to understand how the Internet works the telephone system is not a good analogy. The telephone system is a *circuit switched*

---

[10] Commercial telecommunication companies providing WAN connections include BT, Mercury, AT&T, France Telecom, etc.

network, which means that if you dial someone and make a connection, no one else can dial that person until you finish the conversation. No one else can contact you or the other end. Your connection is 'frozen'.

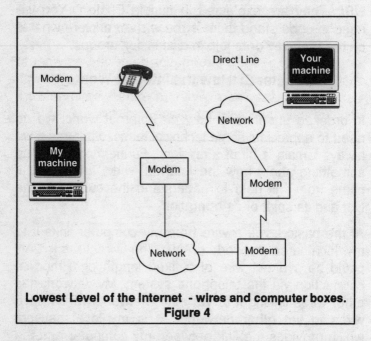

Lowest Level of the Internet - wires and computer boxes.
Figure 4

A better analogy is the postal system which is a *packet switched* network. Information is sent in envelopes and many people all over the country can drop their letters in the post box at the same time. More important, is that all of them can be forwarded to the same address and arrive on the same day. Other letters do not have to wait until one letter is sent and received before the next letter is allowed to be sent. No one person can, therefore, hog the entire network. We can all share the service and all at the same time. Let us relate this to the Internet.

Figure 5 shows three networks. One is a university campus-wide network using, say, an Ethernet connection,[11] another is a company network, possibly built around a token ring configuration. The third is the regional and national telephone network. Note that there is another set of boxes called *routers*. It is these routers which forward information from one network to another and thus connect a user at one site with another user elsewhere. Without routers each network would remain independent, alone.

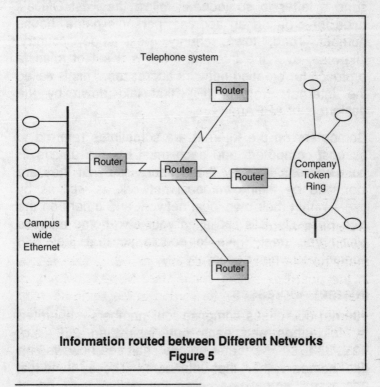

Information routed between Different Networks
Figure 5

---

[11] An Ethernet is one type of network. A token ring is another.

Routers, then, connect networks together. They are computers which know about other routers in their vicinity. When I send information to somewhere beyond my company's network, it is forwarded to my local router. This one decides which of all the routers it knows about is the best one to forward my data to so that it can more quickly arrive at its destination. In order for the router to make such a decision, I must include the address of the machine to which I wish to send my information. The router needs to look at the address before making its decision.

This is what our local postmaster does. When I wish to send a letter to someone, I follow the Post Office's rules for creating an address: person's name, house number, road, town, county, post code, country. Likewise, over the Internet, there is a set of rules (*a protocol*) for creating network addresses. This is called the Internet Protocol (IP), first laid down by the designers of ARPAnet.

Computers on the Internet are sometimes referred to as *host* computers and each must have a unique IP host address. It is by these addresses that they are identified by their own local network as well as by users within their own local network and others on the Net. Basically, it is similar to your own home address which you freely give to people so that they can contact you when necessary.

Internet Addresses

Internet addresses comprise four numbers, separated by full stops and each one less than 256, e.g. `122.234.34.8`. (Later on, we shall see how we can use names rather than numbers.) These numerical addresses, sometimes called the *dotted-quad*, go at the start of your information. The leftmost part tells the router which network you are part of, the right section tells the router which computer should receive that information. Clearly, no two computers should have the same address.

Obviously, the router needs programs to allow it to make all these decisions and to decipher addresses. This is what is known as the IP software and it sits on top of the basic wires, rather like one onion ring sits on top of another. See Figure 6.

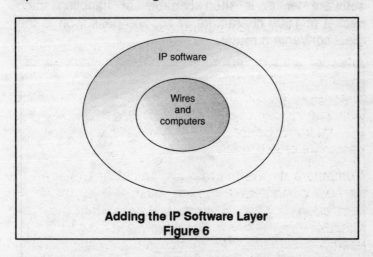

Adding the IP Software Layer
Figure 6

For technical reasons beyond the scope of this book, the data sent over IP networks (i.e. those networks which subscribe to this addressing technique) is limited to 1500 characters. Naturally, many people want to send or receive much more than 1500 characters, little more than about 20 lines of text. This is handled by the TCP, Transmission Control Protocol, yet another outer layer of the network onion, see Figure 7. It is this layer which prevents the system being monopolised by a handful of users.

Transmission Control Protocol (TCP)

TCP is so closely related to the Internet Protocol that you may often hear people refer to the TCP/IP. Suppose you have a ten page document to send to someone. You will type the document and address it. It is sent off via the network. However the IP cannot handle it, it is too large. The TCP, however can, and it will rip this document into shreds (called *packets*), each of 1500 characters. It will number each one and put on the IP address. Each packet is passed to the IP software which is then capable of handling each packet of 1500 characters or so, and pass it on to the most convenient router.

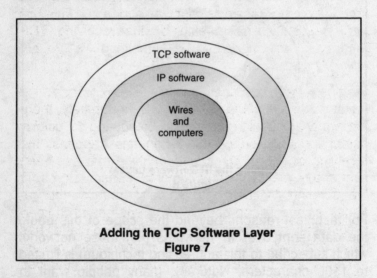

TCP software

IP software

Wires and computers

Adding the TCP Software Layer
Figure 7

When all the packets eventually arrive at the other end and possibly out of order, that network's TCP program will begin to put them together as a single document and in the right order based on the sequence numbers put on by the original TCP software.

My packets of data/information are mixed up with everyone else's packets, just like letters being placed in a post-bag. It is through the IP address and the TCP sequence number that the TCP software at the local network sorts out all the individual packets. All those for Ms Y are put into one mailbox, those for Mr X go into another mailbox. Then, when Ms Y asks for her "mail", they can be sent to her in the correct sequence, from her own mailbox.

To users, exactly what the TCP does is effectively invisible (*seamless* is the jargon term). I send a message, a three page document to Ms Y. She sees a three page document on her computer screen. The fact that during transmission it was ripped into little bits (packets) and re-assembled by the receiving TCP program at the other end, is something we are not normally aware of.

Suppose one of the packets gets lost during transmission, which is not unusual? Fortunately, there are various techniques used in computing to quickly detect transmission errors. When this happens, the receiving computer discards everything that has been sent and requests another complete transmission from the sending machine[12]. Eventually, one of the re-transmissions will be correct. Both ends need to keep in contact until the receiving end is satisfied that all has been received. This is a vast improvement on the manual postal system in which when a letter gets lost, it frequently stays lost.

All this shredding into packets, counting up to 1500 characters, staying in touch until the error detection

---

[12] This proves to be more reliable than the postal service which cannot request another 'transmission' of your letter.

activity is satisfied, adds an overhead to the overall speed at which data is sent and received. Should you need to send less than 1500 characters, then TCP can be slow. However, it has a cousin called UDP, User Datagram Protocol. If, for example, you want to find someone's telephone number, probably less than 20 characters, your application program can use UDP.

UDP

UDP sends a message via the IP as usual but without any frills. If the message gets through to the other end, your computer will eventually receive your requested telephone number and all is well. It can be passed to your display screen. If it does not arrive within a given time period, your program will request the transmission again, having assumed it has been lost. This process will continue until you see the telephone number displayed on to your screen.

That basically is how the Internet works. If you were clever enough and patient enough, few of us are, you could use the Internet just at the IP level. It is all there. But suppose you would like a simpler and easier method of using the Internet, a more user-friendly approach, then you will have to start adding yet other layers to the Internet, one of them being the use of names rather than numbers for addresses. This is the purpose of *domain names*.

Domain Names

If you want to use names, you can do so. The name will need to be turned into an IP numerical address by your local network software in order to travel over the Internet.

Your computer will look up the corresponding numeric address. The number would then be used in place of the name you used. (We do the same when searching for someone's telephone number.)

In the early days, when the number of users on the Internet was manageable, it was the Network Information Centre (NIC) which handled names. It set up a registry. People applied to NIC with their names and IP addresses and were added to the list. This list, called a *hosts' file*, was distributed regularly to all users, rather like a public telephone directory. However, as the number of users grew, it no longer became practical to use the NIC service. There were delays in registering and distributing the name/address file. Some other system was required, this was the on-line Domain Name System. See Figure 8.

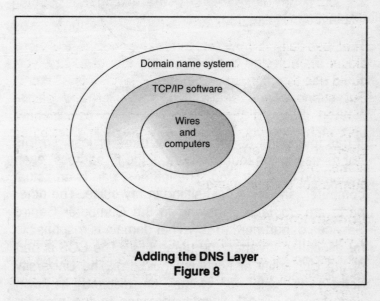

Adding the DNS Layer
Figure 8

Each domain is given the responsibility for creating names within its own group. This will become clearer if we look at an example, albeit fictitious:

`js.ccs.umich.edu` Figure 9 shows the domain structure pictorially for this particular address.

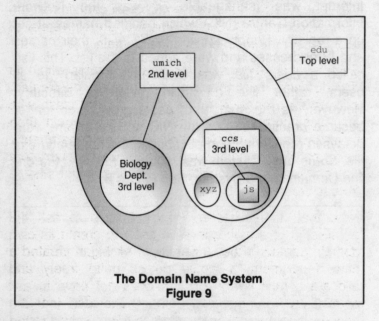

The Domain Name System
Figure 9

It has four parts (there could be more or less, so it is not related to the four numbers of the IP address) each separated by a full stop. The leftmost part is an actual computer, say mine (`js`) sitting in my office. The other parts are *domains*. I belong to the Computer Centre Services department (`ccs`). That domain is responsible for allocating my machine name (`js`). The CCS is part of the University of Michigan (`umich`). The University domain is able to create or disband its own departments. The University belongs to the main or higher edu[13] domain, standing for educational organisations.

The *edu*, then, is the overall domain for all educational computers in the States. The domain *umich.edu* contains all the computers in the University of Michigan. The domain *ccs.umich.edu* contains all the computers in the CCS department of the University of Michigan, in the main educational domain.

Each level is responsible for creating names within its own domain. Thus, should a new university be created, *edu* would allocate a name which did not clash with any existing name. The new university would then have to create names for each of its own departments, being careful to make each unique. Each department would in turn be responsible for creating unique names for each of its computers.

Note that a lower level does not have to ask the permission of a higher level in order to create its own domain names. If the University of Michigan created a new department, it would do so quite freely and allocate a new name for it. It does not have to ask permission from the *edu* domain. Provided that the new department makes its address-name known to the outside world, say on headed notepaper, then others can begin to make contact with it over the Internet. Many people are now adding their Internet address to their business cards and notepaper, either as a new company joining the Internet or as a single home user.

If CCS decides to buy another computer, it does so. The local domain administrator of CCS simply allocates a unique name for it, (say, xyz). This new name (xyz.ccs.umich.edu) is made known to the

---

[13] See Table 1 for the other five main domain names.

outside world by its owner and it is now on the Internet. There was no need to get 'permission' from anyone else in the University or from *edu*. Usually, each domain appoints one person to look after the allocation of names within that domain.

It is often possible to make out where a computer resides if you know to what the individual domain names refer. There are six main domain names used in the States, see Table1:

Domain Name	Refers to
com	commercial organisations (co in UK)
edu	educational institutions; universities, schools, etc. (ac in UK)
gov	government non-military organisations
mil	military (army, navy, air-force, etc.)
net	network resources
org	other non-profit organisations which do not fit into any of the other categories

Table 1

A similar naming system is used in e-mail addresses, especially outside the US - doc.ic.ac.uk - for example: refers to the Department of Computing (doc) at Imperial College (ic) which belongs to the academic community (ac) in the United Kingdom (uk). The last part of the host name usually denotes the country code, although by tradition it is usually omitted for the States. Table 2 lists some other countries.

Code	Country	Code	Country
au	Australia	nl	The Netherlands
br	Brazil	no	Norway
ca	Canada	nz	New Zealand
fi	Finland	es	Spain
fr	France	se	Sweden
il	Israel	ch	Switzerland
jp	Japan	us	United States

Table 2

It is now time to add another layer of software. So far, we have learnt about the address system used on the Internet. But now it is time to actually do something a little more useful. Table 3 illustrates the four main activities which those who are on the Internet perform.

Activity	Explanation
E-mail	to send messages to others and to hold discussions
newsgroups	an alternative form of discussion for specialist interest groups
finding information	special programs are used to find and retrieve information
retrieving files	having found something of interest, you may wish to transfer it to your own computer

Table 3

Chapter 6: Using the Internet

There are two basic tools (application programs, if you prefer) which allow work to be done on the Internet. These are *ftp* and *telnet*. The lowercase is deliberate, that is how they are usually written. Other tools can send electronic mail (e-mail) and access information supplied by newsgroups. Yet others, such as *gopher* or *Archie*, help users to find information. The latest and most sophisticated tool for finding and retrieving information is called the World Wide Web (Figure 10). We shall begin with e-mail.

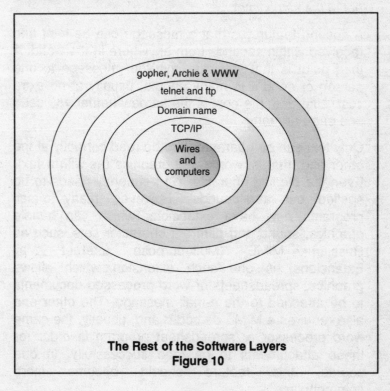

The Rest of the Software Layers
Figure 10

E-Mail

One highly popular activity on the Internet is sending electronic mail or e-mail as it is frequently called. This dates back even to the early days of the ARPAnet. There are several features of e-mail which make it so attractive. First, you can type your message and send it off but the person at the other end does not have to be there in order to receive it, nor does his or her computer have to be switched on. Those who are sent e-mail can log on to their computer network at a later time and 'collect' their mail messages. This is called *asynchronous communication* (from the Greek meaning: *not at the same time*).

A second feature, is that a message can be sent and received within seconds from anywhere in the world. A third point is that you can limit your message to one person or send it to many people, usually at no extra cost. Likewise, the cost is the same whether you send one page or many.

Only text can be guaranteed to be read correctly at the other end, that is, words, not graphics (as with a fax). Even the sterling character (£) frequently needs to be spelled out as 'pounds'. However, many e-mail programs now have extensions which can handle graphics, sound and different character sets, such as Russian. MIME (Multi-purpose Internet Mail Extensions) is one such extension which allows graphics, spreadsheets or word processed documents to be attached to the e-mail message. The other end also requires a MIME de-coder and, usually, the same word processor or spreadsheet program in order for these attachments to be read successfully. In due course, this feature should become more commonplace.

Who Can I contact?

Literally anyone or any organisation connected to the Internet provided you know the address, as well as all those on your own local network; you can even contact those in the Outernet.

Outernets

There are a number of very large world-wide networks which do not use the TCP/IP address system. These are outside the Internet. Some examples are CompuServe, Bitnet, UUCP, Delphi, see Table 4. But seeing how useful the Internet has become, they wish to be connected to the Internet, see Figure 11. It is quite common to express all the world wide networks as clouds, simply because their network inter-connections are too complicated to show in detail.

Name	Type of Organisation
CompuServe	commercial network
Genie	commercial network
BITNET	academic & research network
UUCP	Unix to Unix Copy Protocol, a collection of dial up connections
DELPHI	commercial but offering full Internet services

Table 4

Due to the different protocols each outernet uses, it is difficult to share in their separate services. Currently, the only service that can be guaranteed is e-mail. Each network has a computer which can translate between its own protocol and that of the Internet; these are known as *e-mail gateways* or *bridges*.[14] Thus, e-mail messages can be sent not only throughout the Internet but further beyond to the Outernets.

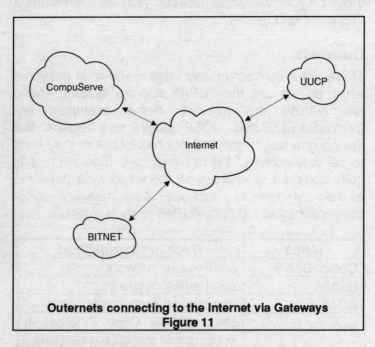

**Outernets connecting to the Internet via Gateways
Figure 11**

The e-mail Address

It consists of two parts, separated by the @ symbol:

`username@hostname`

The `username` (defined by the local network administrator) specifies the person to whom you are sending the message, `f.bloggs`. Case is not usually relevant but it is safer to use lowercase because many

---

[14] These gateways are sometimes called Mail Exchange (MX) computers. They connect to the Internet and convert between address protocols.

networks are Unix workstations which historically use the Unix convention of lowercase letters.[15]

The `hostname` part is the domain name as discussed earlier in Chapter 5.

Thus: `f.bloggs@ic.ac.uk` means the address of F.Blogg's machine, at Imperial College (`ic`) which is part of the academic community (`ac`) in the United Kingdom (`uk`). Such a short and simple address will reach F.Bloggs from anywhere in the world! Let us say you are in Australia. The `uk` part will forward the message through international networks to the UK. At the UK end, a router will select the Academic Community's 'directory' and send the message to Imperial College (`ic`). Imperial College's network knows all the people (machines) at `ic`, including Fred Bloggs. Incidentally, the way to say the above address is: "f dot bloggs at ic dot ac dot uk"

How to Find Someone's e-mail Address

Unfortunately, there is no huge Internet directory. Different networks have their own limited directories and the more you use the Internet, the more of these you may come across. Sometimes the only way to find someone's e-mail address is either to write to them or telephone (sad really!) or look at their headed notepaper or business cards. Hence, the tendency today to add one's e-mail address along with one's telephone number and postal address.

---

[15] The reason being that earlier terminals, back in 1969, could support only uppercase characters. Later models had both lower and upper case characters. Today, if you login to a Unix network in uppercase, the Unix system may think you are still using one of the very early models and treat you as though you were a second class citizen.

What do I need to send e-mail and what can I do?

- a PC or Mac
- access to a LAN (Local Area Network) which in turn has access to the Internet
- network software to connect to your local network
- an e-mail program, such as Eudora[16] for the PC or Mac, or some other proprietary e-mail program
- your own e-mail address

You tell your own network administrator that you have an e-mail package and would like to send and receive e-mail. The administrator will supply you with your own unique address. Then, you let the world know your e-mail address. Remember that your e-mail is delivered to your machine, like letters being delivered to your own home letter box. Anyone who can use your machine can pick up your mail.

What does e-mail offer?

Essentially, send and receive mail messages.

Retrieving Your Mail

When you call up your e-mail program, it will connect to the local postmaster on which your mail is stored in your absence. The program will retrieve (collect) your mail and store it on your own machine's hard disc. It will then display the messages so that you can read them on your own computer screen.

Since the mail is stored on your own hard disc, once it has been collected from the local postmaster, you can

---

[16] Eudora is very easy to use, has a Windows and a Mac environment and is free! Others are Microsoft Mail, Pegasus Mail, etc.

read it at your leisure. If you need to reply to a particular message, you click (with a mouse) on a *reply button*, type in your reply and send it off by clicking on a *send button*. If you have not seen one of these programs before, they are surprisingly easy to use.

All e-mail messages have two parts, a *header* and a *body*, see Figure 12. In the header you type in three things: to whom the message is to be sent; any carbon copies and blind copies[17]; and a short subject description. The e-mail program adds to this when the message is sent, such as your e-mail address and your full name, the date and time and your signature.

TO: f.bloggs@ic.ac.uk   *(Header Part)*
FROM: j.smith@ncl.ac.uk
SUBJECT: IEEE Summer Conference
CC:
BCC:
                                                   (Body Part)
I am pleased to enclose details of the 1996 Summer IEEE conference to be held at ..... etc.

Best Wishes
John Smith
IEEE Conference Organiser

Header & Body of a typical E-Mail Message
Figure 12

You then type in your message in the body part and click the *send* button when you have finished. The e-mail program will add its own information and deliver it

---

[17] The receiver of the message will be able to see the names of people who will receive carbon copies, but not those to whom you have sent blind carbon copies.

to the local postmaster who then forwards it to the address.

Most e-mail programs have *reply*, *send* and *forward* buttons. If you have read a message and decide it should be forwarded to someone else you click the forward button, type in the address and click the send button.

You can also send the same message to a group of people, and at no extra cost. Many e-mail programs allow you to create a list of addresses and then allow you to give a single name to that list. When that name is used in the *To: box* in the e-mail header, the message will be sent to all the people (machines) on the list. For example, a group named staff-cc may include all members of staff in the Computer Centre; safeofficers may be a group name for all the Safety Officers in an organisation. The message is typed, the group name typed into the *To: box* and all staff or safety officers will receive the same message.

Generally speaking, only text can be sent in an e-mail message. Unlike a fax, no graphics can be included nor bold, tabs, underlines, italics, fancy looking fonts, etc. This is because e-mail recognises just plain text, known as ASCII (American Standard Code for Information Interchange). It is a common code which all computers can recognise. Yes, things are changing and some e-mail programs can recognise other forms of codes, even documents created on standard word processors. However, it is no good sending such a message unless you know that the person at the other end has a similar e-mail program and perhaps the same word processor as you have. For the moment, the only thing you can *guarantee* is that ASCII text will be received in a readable if plain format by all computers.

Empty the Trash-Bin

One thing e-mail users need to do from time to time is to delete unwanted mail from their hard discs. All received messages are usually stored in an IN directory,[18] all messages you send out, reply to or forward to others are stored in an OUT directory. All deleted messages are stored in what many e-mail programs call the TRASH directory. If you do not do some housekeeping from time to time, all these messages will accumulate until you run out of disc space. Unwanted files need to be deleted regularly.

E-Mail Discussion Groups

When you become an e-mail user, you can communicate easily with groups of people who share your particular interests. You send messages back and forth to each other. There are interest groups for practically everyone; business, academia, games, humour, research, recreation, hobbies, fringe groups, etc., etc. When you join (*subscribe to*) a group, you will begin to receive messages from that group and you can begin to join in or simply remain a *lurker*. A lurker is the term used for someone who likes to browse or listen to the discussions without actually taking part in the discussions. It is not a derogatory term.

---

[18] A directory (or a folder on the Mac) is a part of a hard disc where computer files are stored. You can have as many directories as you wish. Each one is rather like a separate drawer in a filing cabinet where related information is kept.

How Do I Subscribe?

Simply send an e-mail message to the person who maintains that particular discussion group. Usually, that person's address is quite separate from the actual mailing list of members. A typical example, though fictitious, for a group discussing roses, would be:

```
roses-request@roses.org
```

The `-request` is a common Internet method of sending your e-mail to the group list administrator. However, that person must read your mail and add your name to the mailing list. People are human and do not always do what they should. Consequently, automated packages were developed so that when requested these computer programs would add your name to a list automatically. One of the earliest of these packages was written for BITNET, an educational community on the Outernet but now linked via a gateway to the Internet. The program was called *listserv.* It proved popular and many other variations were developed: *mailserv, majordomo, almanac*.

To subscribe to the roses-group, if it were automated using **listserv**, you would send the message: `subscribe roses yourname` (in the body part of the e-mail message) to: `listserv@roses.org` (in the header's To: box).

Now, the burning questions are: how do you find out which discussion groups are available and what method is used to subscribe to them? Well that has become a problem, there are so many groups and no one central index. In Chapter 7, under the World Wide Web, we discuss ways of finding out what groups are available. There is a short list given in Appendix A.

Newsgroups

One of the attractions of the Internet, especially to beginners, is the news or discussion facility. You may have a question to ask or an interest in an obscure or not so obscure hobby. The Internet allows you to ask your question or discuss your hobby with the entire world (this is known as *conferencing*). It may appear similar to e-mail but there are differences which are discussed later.

It may come as a surprise to discover that newsgroups actually pre-date the Internet from as early as the 1970s. As networks developed, people on those networks created *newsgroups*, sometimes called Bulletin Board Systems, essentially articles written by a group of people interested in a particular subject. These articles were then sent (*posted*) to newsgroup sites where they were made available, free of charge.

There are many different networks which generate and pass on their newsgroup articles. Some are created by large academic institutions, some by commercial companies, others by government bodies, fringe groups, etc. Anyone can contribute to these discussions.

To take part in newsgroups you require a *newsreader* program. This in turn is linked to a *news server* which, by arrangement, is fed news by certain newsgroups. Which newsgroups your network has access to depends on the local network administrator's overall policy. Your company boss may not wish staff members to join in discussions about art and music whilst at work. Likewise, academic institutions may prefer their staff to concentrate on academic work. But in any case, the volume of news is so vast that many networks would become overloaded and probably run out of disc space if they subscribed to all of them. One is forced to become selective.

USENET

USENET (Users' Network) is a world wide system for distributing and allowing participation in discussion groups (newsgroups). It allows like-minded people to gather together to discuss the subjects closest to their hearts. There are currently more than 12,000 newsgroups. Via your newsreader you are linked to a news server which is fed news (*feeds*) by certain sites. These sites collect news and distribute it to those news servers with which it has agreements. (See Figure 13.)

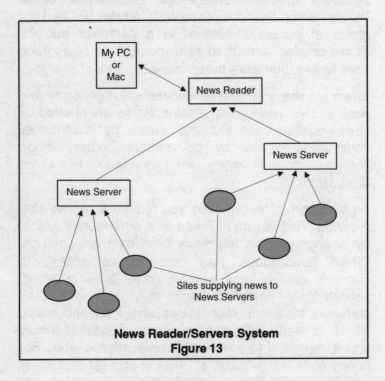

News Reader/Servers System
Figure 13

Figure 14 illustrates a newsreader collecting news not only from USENET but also from several other similar systems, such as Clarinet and a local news source. There is also a *mail reflector* which forwards e-mail discussion groups. A mail reflector is a special mail address. E-mail sent to this address is automatically forwarded to a set of other addresses, typically a particular discussion group. There are many different systems in use, USENET being but one.

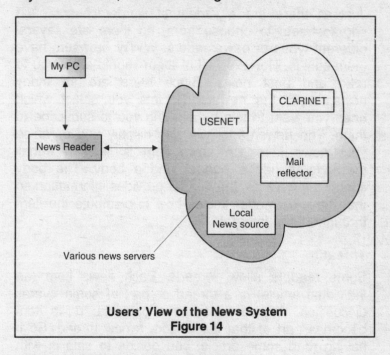

Users' View of the News System
Figure 14

What do I need to join in USENET?

- a PC or Mac (or Unix workstation, etc.)
- access to a LAN (Local Area Network) which in turn has access to the Internet[19]

---

[19] Not strictly true, see 'What USENET is and what it is not'.

49

- communications software to connect to your local network
- a newsreader program to read or post news (these are built into WWW browsers, such as Netscape, Cello, etc.)
- a local network administrator who allows access to USENET via a news server

Newsreaders

Just as there are a variety of wordprocessors and spreadsheets to choose from, so there are several different types of newsreaders. WWW browsers have them built in. However, all of them should allow you to read and post news. Since there are so many newsgroups, the newsreader lets you select which ones you want to join by allowing you to subscribe to them. The newsreader will also display and organise your news items. A news item is like an e-mail message, it has a header and a body. The body contains the article, the header provides information so that the newsreader knows how to distribute the item throughout the Internet.

Threads

Some readers allow *threads*. Each news item (an individual article) is a thread or part of some overall discussion. Any response to a particular news item becomes part of that discussion, a new thread. So if having read some article, you decide to chip in with your two-pennies worth of opinion, that becomes another thread in the overall discussion. Newsreaders which allow threads are useful since you can see what new articles have been posted about the particular discussion you are interested in and those which you have already seen.

What USENET is and what it is not

It is worthwhile to know exactly what USENET is. We shall start by saying what it is not. It is not the Internet. The Internet is but one of the many world-wide networks which carry USENET news. It is not an organisation since no one person or group has authority over USENET. It is not a network of any description (although some articles imply this). It is not a software package, although a variety of software programs at different sites are designed to carry USENET news. So, if it is not hardware or software, what is it? People!

USENET is the set of people who exchange articles (newsgroups) and abide (mainly) by a set of codes. You can become part of USENET by posting articles for USENET readers to read. Each administrator controls his or her own network site. So the control over what goes into USENET depends upon the policy of each local administrator.

USENET Categories

The variety of newsgroups is so vast that some sort of categorisation is essential. Knowing what these categories mean will give you some indication of the general content of the newsgroups. USENET has seven major categories, see Table 5. A number of alternative top level categories also exist, see Table 6. Within each category, further sub-divisions exist which describe exactly what the discussion is about; for example, see whether you work these out, if you can, you will find *surfing* easy:

```
talk.rights.human    alt.sport.hockey
rec.music.folk       rec.humor.funny[20]
```

---

[20] You may need to adjust to American spelling.

Major Categories	Explanation
comp	computer hardware, software, languages, topics of general interest
news	groups which deal with USENET software, network administration, questions from new users, information for new users. A good place to start for beginners, see Appendix A.
rec	recreational activities and hobbies such as cooking, games, etc., the arts
sci	groups discussing scientific research in many subjects apart from computer science; ranges from popular to research level
soc	groups discussing social issues, socialising, world culture and current events
talk	lengthy debates and discussions on various current affairs and issues - politics, religion, environment, etc. They tend to be long winded and unresolved and sometimes of great interest
misc	topics that do not fit into any of the above categories

Table 5

Alternative Categories	Explanation
alt	many frivolous, controversial, bizarre groups here with an alternative way of looking at things; definitely not mainstream and unpalatable to some; however, there are some important groups as well, e.g. gopher
bionet	for research biologists
biz	business and commercial topics
clari	commercial news services from ClariNet
de	recreational, social and technical topics in German
gnu	discussions about Free Software
ieee	about IEEE (Institute of Electronic and Electrical Engineers)
info	a group of mailing lists covering a wide range of topics
relcom	Russian language newsgroups (special software is required to display the Cyrillic alphabet)

Table 6

When to Use USENET or e-mail for discussions

If you use e-mail for discussions with other people, your machine will receive everything that comes. You will need to read it and/or, at the very least, delete any unwanted messages from your hard disc. These discussions will also be mixed up with all your normal business mail. On the other hand, if you use USENET, then you can browse at your own leisure and dip into articles that look interesting and, if *you* wish, store them on your hard disc. Those which do not inspire you can be ignored completely. If you do not wish to participate any more, then do not. You will not be bombarded with unwanted 'mail' as you would with e-mail.

However, because of the sheer volume of traffic on USENET, administrators will usually have to clear off articles at given times, perhaps weekly! You can therefore easily miss something of interest. With e-mail, you can collect your mail after your summer break and store it on your hard disc for as long as you want. It all comes down to *compromise*, a word which for me sums up what computing is frequently all about.

Finding Information

One of the main problems we all have is trying to find out whether some information exists and if so where it is. It is an ever-growing problem. The Internet is so vast and there are so many pools of information that it became necessary to create special programs to help us find what we want. Archie, gopher, Veronica, WAIS and, latterly, World Wide Web programs are some of the tools which have been invented.

Today, many of us use one of the WWW programs to help us find information. It is therefore not necessary to know much about the earlier programs except that since their names crop up all over the place you may find it interesting to know a little about them. Chapter 8 discusses some of these earlier Internet tools.

For the moment, we shall move straight on to the World Wide Web since this is fast becoming the most popular tool for finding information on the Internet.

Chapter 7: The World Wide Web

Not too long ago, working on the Internet to find information, to transfer documents to your computer so that they could be printed, keeping track of what had been read, using e-mail or the USENET discussion groups, etc., was not easy. One had to have a degree of computer expertise in several different program tools. Fortunately today, we no longer need such a level of computing competence because packages have been developed which hide many of the technical niceties. Netscape, Cello and Mosaic, among others, are three such packages. These employ a concept called the World Wide Web, sometimes written as WWW, W3 or W^3. They are often referred to as *browsers* and they use a technique called *hypertext*. These two terms are explained below.

Background to WWW

The concept of the WWW dates back to the 1960s. Ted Nelson, a student at Harvard University, had a vision that one day every citizen would have instant access to information via computer screens. Not just text but a full hypermedia system involving sound, images, films and so forth just by clicking on an icon.

But it was some three decades before the technology caught up with the vision. In 1989, Tim Berners Lee proposed a WWW project for communicating ideas between high energy physicists at the CERN laboratory in Switzerland. Today, we can all share in the World Wide Web concept.

Basically, the WWW is a browsing and searching system. It allows us to explore the Internet's world wide network of information (the Web). The information is put up on the Web by individual network sites. Just what is stored at these local sites depends upon the people in charge of the networks. It is their choice. The information on the Web is, therefore, stored in many different centres and it is growing by the minute.

The Web is a concept, like word processing. To perform word processing one must have a particular word processor, such as WordPerfect 6 for Windows, Ami Pro, Word 6, etc. Likewise, packages such as Netscape permit us to explore the World Wide Web. It is based on a concept called *hypertext*. The packages are known as browsers[21].

Hypertext

Imagine you are in a library, searching a card index system for a particular book. When you find the card it will contain details such as the book title, shelf position, author, publisher, date of publication, etc. Now suppose that you would like to know more about the author. Let us say that you could simply press the author's name on the card and up pops another card with details about the author, including a photograph and details about other books he or she has written. One of these titles interests you and you press on the title. Lo and behold! another card pops up from 'nowhere' with a brief summary of the book, cost, shelf position, and so on. You may now wish to go back to the original card, press on the shelf position, and a map of the library pops up showing you where the

---

[21] Strictly speaking, a browser is any program capable of reading hypertext. Web programs, such as Netscape, are essentially hypertext readers and so they are called browsers.

physical shelf is situated. That is what hypertext is all about.

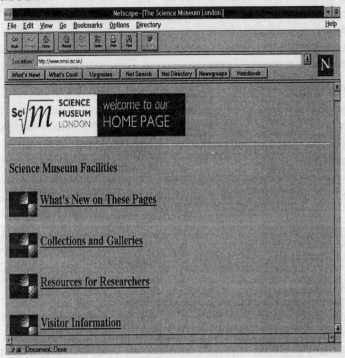

Home Page of the Science Museum, London
Figure 15

When using the WWW, some of the text is in colour, typically blue and frequently underlined as well. This is the actual hypertext itself. See Figure 15. The rest of the text is usually black. When the mouse pointer is moved to a piece of hypertext (or indeed a hypertext image) the arrow changes to a hand with a pointing finger. By clicking on the coloured text or image, another page of information appears providing more detail about that text or picture. In turn, this page may have yet other coloured hypertext. By clicking on another hypertext phrase, yet another page of information pops up telling you all about that text. When you have finished, you can click on a button which will take you back to the start - note the Back & Forward buttons at the top in the Figure on page 66.

It is really quite a simple concept. The coloured text, usually a word or short phrase, or even a picture, has a link to another document which provides more detail about that word or phrase or image. That other document is often simply a separate file, stored on the network's discs, but it could equally well be at any other site in the Internet. When you click on the word, the system is set up to search for that document and to display it on the screen. The link, called a *hyper-link*, is really an address where the document is stored. (It is rather like someone using Windows or the Mac operating system to *open* a file, which has been previously stored on their computer's hard disc. The link is merely an address of where that document is held. (See Figure 16.) In Chapter 9, we explain briefly the means whereby you can create your own hypertext documents and create hypertext links.

Home Pages

When you call up your WWW package, there is a set page of information which you always see, although it can be changed at any time. This *home page*, as it is called, is usually prepared by the local network you are 'visiting'. It is their home page. Typically, this will consist of a short introduction and a list of words or phrases rather like the menu in Figure 15. The intention is to invite you to read about their particular organisation.

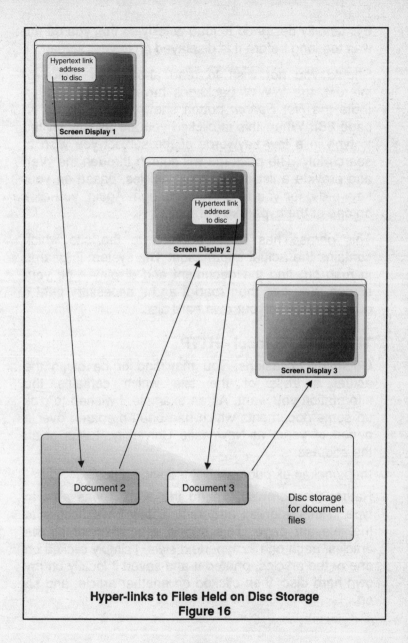

Hyper-links to Files Held on Disc Storage
Figure 16

It is usually designed to load quickly so that you do not wait too long before it is displayed on to your screen.

Should you not wish to read about their topics of interest, the WWW packages have a search button (note the *Net Search* button shown in the Figure on page 66). When this is clicked you are usually invited to type in a few keywords of the subject you wish to search for. The package will search through the Web and provide a list of hypertext articles, based on your keywords, for you to browse through. Again, you click on one of the hypertext phrases.

This phrase has a link-address to the site which contains the actual information. The system is geared to rush off, find the document and display it on your screen. You can then read it and if necessary print it out or store it on your own hard disc.

The WWW Protocol - HTTP

On many occasions, you may find or be given the actual address of the site which contains the information you want. As an example, I wished to pick up some documents which had been prepared over a period of years at Newcastle University. I was given the address:

(http://ncl.ac.uk/pub/network-training/trainpack)

Rather than browse around the Web, I was able to type in this address and immediately have access to the relevant page. This had a description of all the articles, each one in hypertext style. I simply clicked on one of the articles, printed it and saved it locally on my own hard disc; then clicked on another article, and so on.

HTTP and URL

On page 66, there is a box after the word Location. It is in here that you can type in addresses. An address consists of three parts:[22]

- *a resource descriptor*, i.e. which protocol is being used to transfer data. The one for hypertext is *http* (HyperText Transport Protocol). `http` refers to the type of server on which the information is stored, namely, WWW hypertext documents. We shall see later that the WWW browsers can handle many other types of server protocols as well.

- *a separator*, which consists of a colon and two forward slashes - `://`

- everything which follows is the *address* where the resource is stored. By resource, we mean documents, sound, images, etc. The following example gives the address for the Web's own daily cartoon - Doctor Fun (©David Farely).

Example:

`http://sunsite.unc.edu/Dave/drfun.html`

`http`   specifies a WWW hypertext server

`://`   is the separator

`sunsite.unc.edu/Dave/` is the site location and
                  directory of where the resource is stored

`drfun.html` is the name of the resource - a cartoon
                  in this case

---

[22] Case, upper and lower letters, is significant in these addresses.

Note the `.html`. This stands for HyperText Markup Language, the language in which hypertext documents are created (see Chapter 9). The whole line is called the URL - Universal Resource Locator - and means exactly what it says: the location of where the resource is stored in the Universe, the Universe here being the Internet. It is becoming the standard way of addressing Internet resources.

Another Example: `http://www.scifi.com`

Here the actual resource document is omitted. Your browser will contact the site - `www.scifi.com` - using the WWW http protocol. The site will provide a page of information, rather like a home page, from which you can select the topic of interest. From the example, you ought to make out that it is concerned with Science Fiction (`scifi`) and, because of the `com`, one of the main domains in the US, refers to companies.

To summarise, when you click on a piece of hypertext, the WWW browser (the client) sends off a request to the WWW site (the server) pointed to in the URL address using the http protocol.

Search and Find Tools

Before World Wide Web browsers became a reality, and by that I mean hypertext browsers, two basic tools were used: *ftp* and *telnet*. telnet allowed a person at one site to make use of facilities present at some other site. For example, from my office micro in London, I could *telnet* to a network site in the States and perform actions at that site just as if I were one of their local users.

Just what I would be allowed to do at that site would be laid down by the local network administrator. But typically, I could be allowed to browse through and list their files, display them (or those I would be allowed to look at) on my screen, etc. Should I wish to transfer a copy of a file to my local London hard disc, I would have to use the *ftp* (the File Transfer Protocol) program tool.

These were the two basic tools Internet users had to use up to a few years ago, and many still do. One had to learn their different commands and syntax rather like MS-DOS users had to do before Windows arrived. They were not difficult to learn, but it did take time. Consequently, other program tools were developed, such as gopher, Archie, Veronica, WAIS, to make it easier to roam around the Internet. Essentially, they are a combination of the two basic tools plus a little bit more.

gopher, ftp and WWW servers

When information is stored at a site, the person responsible for creating the material has to decide how others are going to access that file. It could be via *ftp*, *gopher* or *http*. If it were a gopher type document, it would be stored on the gopher server (on the disc storage system). An ftp document would be stored on the ftp server, etc. When someone wanted to access that document, he or she would have to know whether to use a gopher or an ftp program. Remember that all these tools are really protocols, rules or methods for accessing the documents.

The beauty about a WWW browser is that it not only knows how to handle its own http protocols but also ftp, gopher, e-mail, etc. By using this one tool you are effectively able to use the others. All you need to do is to precede the document's address with the type of server (the resource descriptor) being used. This is why you will frequently see a variety of URLs:

> ftp://address
> http://address
> gopher://address

You simply type the full address into the URL location box and your WWW browser will perform all the necessary actions on your behalf which previously you would have had to learn and do for yourself.

Client-Server

The way these tools work is based on a *Client-Server* model. The client may be your computer network or your WWW browser, depending on what activity you are performing. Its purpose is to request some service, on your behalf, from some distant computer. The distant computer is the *server*, a provider of certain services, see Figure 18.

The client has software which:

- creates a TCP/IP network connection with a distant server
- accepts your message requesting some service
- reformats the request into a standard form and sends it to the server
- accepts output from the server and reformats the output so that you can read it

The server has software which:

- informs the network software that it is ready to accept connections from other sources
- waits for a request (which must be in a standard format which it can understand)
- services the request

- sends the results back to the client, again in a standard format
- waits for another request

If the server is not running, you cannot get any service. (Unix servers are often called *daemons*.)

There are many different types of client computers, PCs, Macs, Unix, IBM mainframes, etc., as well as program tools. Clearly, there must be a standard set of rules which all these different machines and programs must adhere to if they want to be able to talk to one another. These rules are called *protocols*. If the client speaks the same protocol as the server, the server knows what the client is requesting.

What these Browsers have to offer

- hypertext; hypermedia: sound, movies, images. You will need a full multi-media computer system to enjoy sound and movies and a huge storage system. Chapter 10 discusses the hardware requirements in more detail
- security; fill-in forms. This allows you to go shopping and even buy goods directly with your credit cards on the Internet. However, you should be aware of the security aspects, see Chapter 11 on security
- e-mail and newsgroups
- adding your annotations and audio annotations to existing Web documents
- finding discussion groups
- saving, printing, remembering where documents are

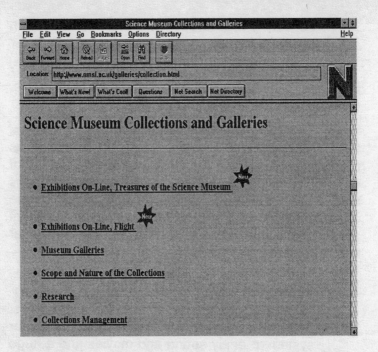

This is the WWW page which was displayed when the
hypertext *Collections and Galleries* was clicked from the
Science Museum's home page in Figure 15.

Figure 17

Chapter 8   Earlier Internet Tools

Some of the earlier tools used for *finding* information on the Internet, and still being used by some people, are discussed here. You will come across references to these tools and for those who would like to know something about them, read on. Remember, however, that WWW browsers incorporate all the various features of these earlier tools.

gopher, Veronica and WAIS

gopher is supposedly a corruption of the phrase *Go for it!* Like all the others, it is a protocol which allows one computer network to access information stored on another computer network. The two computers do not have to be the same, and more than likely are not. Provided both understand the gopher protocols (rules) then they can communicate with each other.

gopher uses menus, hierarchical menus. That is, there is a top menu which provides certain main options. When one of these main options is chosen, another lower level menu pops up and gives you more choices. This goes on until you have found what you are looking for. Then you can ask gopher to retrieve that document for you. Not only text documents but also images and movies can be retrieved.

Veronica was designed to allow *keyword* searching for the rapidly expanding gopher sites. It is used from within gopher, usually an additional item in one of the gopher menus. Its main advantage is that it saves the user stepping down through the levels of menus. You type in a keyword and leave it to Veronica to do all the searching through the various levels of menus.

WAIS , Wide Area Information Servers, is a browsing, searching and retrieval tool but unlike Veronica it searches through the contents of documents, not just their file names or menu titles.

telnet, ftp, anonymous ftp and Archie

telnet and ftp are two basic tools used by the searching and retrieving tools. When accessing information, you may be told to use *telnet* or *ftp* as the means to do so.

Those who want to put information on the Information Superhighway frequently need to use these two programs. *ftp* allows you to send (or receive) information; *telnet* allows you to interact with the machine which stores (holds) your information.

telnet

telnet is a protocol (a set of rules) which allows you to connect your office computer to any other site on the Internet, provided it understands the same protocols. This other computer site could be in the same room, on another floor or in some distant continent. Once you are connected you can access whatever services that computer wants to offer. It is rather like being a guest in someone's home. Whilst you are there, you have the use of your host's facilities or at least those your host specifies. This is why these other computer sites are frequently referred to as the *host computer*. You can execute commands, read catalogues, etc.

You need to have an *account* (see below) on the distant computer in order to access its services. Your network computer is called the *client*. The distant computer is called the *server*. See Figure 18.

telnet then is simply a tool which lets you log in to a remote computer. It is the Internet's remote login protocol. It has a few other features, but is really quite basic. Many books exist which describe how to use telnet. You may also need to find out any specific details relating to your local network.

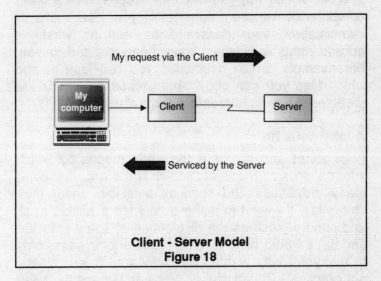

Client - Server Model
Figure 18

ftp

Let us suppose that you have discovered a recipe among all the information on the Superhighway. You would like to print it out on your printer and read it in your kitchen. How do you manage to do this? This is where the *ftp* program comes in. It allows the transfer of files from one computer system to another, provided both have agreed upon a standard protocol.

This program, or perhaps more accurately the protocol, has enabled the creation of databases and other services to be held on servers. Anyone wishing to access the information stored on these servers can do so by using *ftp*. Again, you will need training in how to use *ftp* and each computer system has a slight variation from another. Remember my warning at the start? Some local training, an hour or two, will frequently be required.

In order to use *ftp*, you need an *account* on the other computer. An account consists of your user name or identification, your password as well as whatever access rights (privileges) have been granted to you. For example, which directories you can look at and which files you can copy. *Anonymous ftp* avoids the problem of having to create individual accounts.

Anonymous ftp

Both telnet and ftp were the early means by which information was made available. There are, therefore, many databases and services available under their umbrellas. If I want to make a new file available to all and sundry, such as the distribution of some software update, I would have to also provide login/passwords to everyone who wanted the software. This is clearly not practical. The answer is simply to bypass the need for accounts by using *anonymous ftp*, that is a special login name which anyone can use. Typically, today, this special login name is a person's e-mail name or alternatively the word *anonymous*. The tradition of anonymous ftp grew up because of the academic tradition of giving away certain research papers free. (Not something the market forces people would necessarily approve of today.)

After signing on as *anonymous*, you can access the files permitted to anonymous ftp users.

Archie

There are hundreds of anonymous ftp sites around the world. But how do you find out where they are and what they contain? Enter Archie! Archie is a compiler of lists. It roams around the world collecting lists of the current holdings from anonymous ftp sites. These lists are placed in the Archie database, held in more than fifteen different sites for general public use. When you need to search this database, you give Archie a specified phrase - something you are searching for. In reply, Archie will provide a list of files that match your phrase, their location, and other details required to transfer the files to your computer.

Mirror Sites

One method of speeding up access to information on the Net, especially if it resides in the States, is to duplicate the database site itself. The Department of Computing at Imperial College, London, was one of the first sites to do this by replicating the American SunSite. Instead of having to connect to the States and using the comparatively slow 4Mbit connection along with all the others using the line, one could contact the IC site and enjoy the faster 10Mbit connection. Much more *mirror siting* will have to take place as the demand for access grows. Currently, at any one time there is a 16Mbit traffic waiting to travel down the 4Mbit pipeline.

Such sites need to have their information updated on a regular basis, of course, so that it does not become outdated. But this is usually done at night during off-peak periods.

How to Behave on the Net

A message sent over the Internet could be read by millions of people, of different cultures and language. What you say and how that is interpreted may not be the same. It is easy to annoy others by what you say and how you say it. Likewise, not everyone will share your sense of 'humour'. You can minimise matters by following certain rules, mainly sheer common-sense, which are referred to as *Netiquette*. Here are some of the rules for newsgroup messages, but some apply to e-mail as well.

- Be brief! Long winded messages are seldom read in full and can be boring.
- Keep your line length to about 65 characters, the average readable line-length for computer screens.
- Do not *spam*. Spamming is junk mailing groups of people, say to advertise your product. Some have tried this and found their own system clogged up with *flames* from outraged Net users. A flame is an abusive message from someone you have managed to annoy.
- If you must send a flame, do so via e-mail, not as an open newsgroup message which could start a flame-war.
- Do not shout by overuse of capital letters.
- Keep to a minimum the abbreviations used, e.g. IMHO (in my humble opinion). Better still, never use them.
- If you ask a question, make sure that you have read all relevant FAQs first. Your answer may be one of the Frequently Asked Questions.
- Neatness is important as is grammar and spelling. Sloppy messages stand out and create a bad impression of *you*.
- Do not send a response when you are angry, wait until you have calmed down.
- You do not need to include *Dear Mr X* or *Yours sincerely,* however you should include a signature, but keep it to about 4 lines.

Chapter 9: How to Put Information on to the Highway

Pay Someone

Information on the WWW about your organisation is potentially visible to the whole world. The impression the world gains will depend upon how professional the material looks. A poor impression will be given by an amateurish page of information, a good impression by something that looks smart. If you are not experienced in design features and layout, it is probably better to pay a professional company to mount the pages of information for you. It will not be too expensive, certainly nothing like the cost of advertising in general.

You will probably also need to pay an annual retainer fee to the company so that when your information becomes out of date, the company will update the material. There is no worse impression than old and incorrect details.

Many professionals will use the HyperText Markup Language (HTML) in order to enter the information in a format which the WWW browsers can understand.

Learn HTML

Your second choice is to learn the HTML language yourself so that you can do what the professional can achieve. This too can be expensive, not so much in cost, though you will have to buy books and enrol on courses to learn the language, but more so *in your own time and effort*. Out of interest, Figure 19 shows an HTML document. It includes not only the text which you want others to read but also the codes (the language) which describe or mark up how the text should look - font size, bold, centred, left or right justified, whether it is a paragraph, etc. You need to learn what the codes mean, where and how to insert them, etc.

The codes are inserted between angle brackets (< >) a slash sign means the end of one pair of codes. For example, to italicise an entire phrase, it is encased between a pair of codes:

<I> This bit is in italics </I>

The phrase: 'This bit is in italics' is preceded by the code <I> and what follows will be italicised until the code </I> is encountered by the program (the WWW browser) which will then turn off italic mode. That is a simple example of the use of HTML. Learning all the codes, how to use them (the *syntax*) requires experience and, perhaps, is better left to the professional.

Use Internet Assistant

The third method is fast becoming very common. Word 6 includes a program (the *Internet Assistant* and free at the moment and built into Windows 95) which can automatically insert the language codes for you. Essentially, you write the text and mark phrases as being bold, italic, headings, paragraphs or pictures and the program will insert the necessary codes for you. If you want a phrase to become a hyperlink, it will do all the necessary coding for you.

Internet Assistant, at the time of writing, is only available on Word 6 for Windows (for PCs), it is not yet available on the Macs. It offers a limited number of fonts which are still very acceptable, but for a real professional look the full HTML language is required.

It may be just a matter of time before other word processors will offer similar and perhaps better packages.

```
<!doctype html public "-//IETF//DTD HTML//EN">
<HTML>

<HEAD>

<META      NAME="GENERATOR"      CONTENT="Internet
Assistant for Word 1.00">
<META NAME="AUTHOR" CONTENT="CCS Staff Set">
</HEAD>

<BODY>

<P>
This is John Shelley's Home Page
<P>
And here is information on it.
<P>
<I> This bit is in italics </I>
<P>
<A HREF="group.htm">Return to Group Page here.</A>
</BODY>

</HTML>
```

An Example of the HTML Code
Figure 19

How to Put Images on to the Highway

If you want Auntie Fanny in Canada to know what her latest nephew looks like and to send her a photograph over the Internet, what do you need to do? First get a good photograph of the baby. Yes! an ordinary photograph. Get it developed. When you have your picture, *scan* it into a computerised format. That means, you need to use a *scanner* - a device which will reproduce your picture into a format which a computer can display. These scanners are expensive, so you will probably have to use a commercial company's scanner, at a cost, or make arrangements to use your organisation's scanner, if they have one.

The scanner will convert the photograph into a computerised form as a separate file. This can then be retrieved over the network by Auntie Fanny. Provided she has all the necessary computer equipment (see Chapter 10) she will be able to have a good look at her newphew.

Images tend to be far larger files than mere text files. Consequently, it may take a long time for the data to be sent over the network and for your computer to actually display it on your screen. The faster your micro and your modem (if you need one) are, the more quickly you will receive and display pages of information with pictures in them. Even on a 486 Intel micro, we were not able to give satisfactory Internet courses until the machines had been upgraded to Pentiums. It was taking far too long to wait for images to be seen.

The WWW uses two basic graphic (picture formats) - .GIF (Graphics Interchange Format) & .JPEG (Joint Photographic Experts Group). But it is changing all the time and doubtless other formats will become available. As yet, other formats cannot be converted by WWW programs.

Part C - Social and Practical Issues

Chapter 10:   What Do I Need to Connect to the Internet and the WWW?

This will depend upon what you want to use the Internet for and from where you want to use it. Is it from home or from the office? If you are in a large business or academic organisation, someone else will probably be responsible for installing the appropriate system. You will be told what you will get. So, let us concentrate on the home user and this would include small businesses, societies, even schools. Though in the latter case the local authority, if they are state schools, may be responsible for setting up a system.

Essentially you need three things:

- a computer
- a connection to a network which has links to the Internet
- software with which to use the WWW

The Computer

Most current PCs and Macs are capable of sending e-mail, browsing through the Internet and putting up your own pages of information on the WWW. If you want something more sophisticated, such as sound and video images, you will require a multi-media PC or PowerMac.

Micros vary in price, which in the final analysis means how fast they operate, how much they can store, etc. My own suggestion is that an Intel 486 or Pentium for the PC, or a PowerMac for the Apple Macintosh is required. Anything less powerful can result in having to wait several minutes for images to display onto your screen. A colour monitor would also be required in order to enjoy the Net's coloured text and pictures.

- 486 Intel microprocessor & 33+MHz[24]
- 8 megabytes of RAM - 16 Mbytes is better
- 300 Mb hard disc - minimum

However, if you are thinking of running videos and listening to Rock music, then you enter the multimedia micro market with CD-Roms[25], sound cards and a huge hard disc, say 800 Mbytes. Even this system will not really satisfy your needs. The average office and home user will probably have to await further technological developments before video and sound become easily available on their machines.

Technology is improving all the time and it is more than likely that gadgets will be developed which may do away with the need for home computers in order to link to the Internet. At the time of writing, one company mentions the possibility of a 'black box' for $500 (US) which will allow such a connection and to your TV screen.

The Internet Connection

To use the Internet from home, your computer will need to be linked, via your telephone, to a network which has an Internet connection. Unfortunately,

---

[24] The megahertz speed defines how quickly a microprocessor can execute program instructions. Thus an Intel 486 microprocessor with a 25MHz speed will perform more slowly than a 486 with a 77MHz speed.

[25] A new Super Density disc, SD-Rom, is set to replace the CD-Rom. Capable of holding 4.7 gigabytes of data, equivalent to a full length movie, it has about 8-15 times the capacity of today's CD-Rom.

computer and telephone systems handle information in different ways. Consequently, some device is required to convert between the two formats. This is precisely what a *modem* does. Computers with direct lines linking them to their network, do not require a telephone and modem.

There are many types of modems, so which one should you get? This is not a simple question to answer and needs to be discussed separately below. For the moment we shall discuss where your telephone line leads to.

For those relying purely on a telephone connection, there are many Internet service providers. Some of these are commercial companies who allow access to the Internet via their own network, but for a fee! The services they provide and their pricing systems vary. In addition, you will have to pay for your telephone connect time to these providers. Some organisations, typically in the field of education, may allow local charities and societies to use their network at little or no cost. You usually have to have some personal connection with them, friendly or professional, for them to let you in free. How to choose a service provider, what they have to offer and what they charge is discussed later.

Software Required

Your software could be the very basic tools at a Unix level, but to use them expertise and learning is required. Today, the popular approach is to use one of the WWW browsers. PC users need Windows 3.1 or 95 in order to run a WWW program. If you are using a modem, additional communications software, such as

SLIP or PPP, is required to control the modem. We shall now discuss modems in more detail.

Modems

Why are they needed?

Modems are only required if your Internet connection is via a telephone. The word *modem* is short for **mo***dulator* - **dem***odulator* where modulator refers to the telephone's analogue sound waves.

Information transmitted over telephone lines is in the form of analogue sound waves. Computer information is in a digital format. Both formats are incompatible. A modem converts digital information into an analogue format for transmission over the telephone system and also converts analogue data back into digital data for computer usage. See Figure 20.

To access an Internet Service Provider via a home telephone, one needs:

- an IBM PC, or a Mac, Amiga, Archimedes, Atari, Sun, etc.
- a telephone
- a modem
- communications software
- an RS232 cable

The choice of modem affects the performance and efficiency of your Internet connection. In straightforward terms that means how long you have to wait for a page of information to be transmitted and displayed onto your screen. The same 100K characters[26] could take between 30 seconds and 7 minutes depending on the type of modem you have.

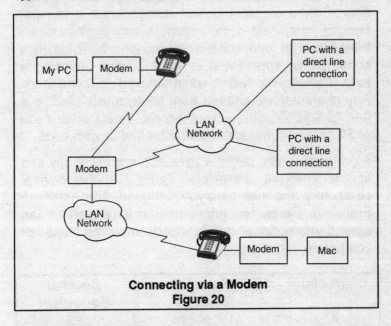

Connecting via a Modem
Figure 20

What type of Modem to Buy

The simplest answer is: "The very best you can afford and perhaps a little bit more." But what does that mean? Perhaps we should be asking: "How can I compare one modem with another?" There are three basic points to look out for:

- speed
- data compression & error correction techniques
- BABT approval

---

[26]   i.e. 100,000 characters (called *bytes*), the average size of a document or image on the Internet. K stands for kilo which is 1024 in computing. So, 100K is really 102,400.

Speed

The basic model is the 2400 bps, so slow that you could find it difficult to buy one today. (There are even slower ones around.) Speed is measured in bits per second (bps), that is, how many **bi**nary *digi**t** s* can be transmitted in one second. Information held inside a computer is represented by binary digits - hence the term *digital information* when applied to computers. Any character we choose from a keyboard, (A-Z, a-z, 0-9, ^&%$£!?>, etc.) is represented by a unique code of 8 bits. Even the space character has its own code.

A group of 8-bits, called a *byte,* can represent any one of 256 different characters. Table 7 shows several characters and their binary ASCII code. The American Standard Code for Information Interchange is an agreed international standard code which all makes of computers can recognise.

Character	ASCII Binary Code (bytes)	Decimal Equivalent
A	01000001	65
B	01000010	66
C	01000011	67
a	01100001	97
b	01100010	98
+	00101011	43
£	01000000	64
space	00100000	32

Table 7

After a few calculations, we can see that a 2400 bps modem could transfer about 300 characters (bytes) per second, roughly 4 lines of normal text.

Such a basic model would permit e-mail, ftp, telnet and WWW browsing. However, in practice, you would be restricted to text. You could also receive pictures but you would need a great deal of patience (and your phone bill would become hefty due to the connection time).

The bigger the file (i.e. the number of bytes) the longer it will take to be transmitted to your computer screen or disc. The faster the modem, the less time it will take and the smaller your telephone bill.

To get the most out of the Net you need a fast modem. 2400 bps is really not adequate today especially since many Internet applications use images. Other speeds are 9600 bps, 14,400 bps and 28,800 bps. The 28,800 bps model is really what is required - certainly by companies and organisations since they can recoup the cost quite quickly by their reduced phone bills. The faster modems also incorporate data compression techniques which help to speed up data transmission.

It is unlikely that modems will get any faster in the foreseeable future, mainly due to the laws of Physics.

What Do they Cost?

- if you can still buy a 2400 bps modem, it will cost about £40 at the time of writing (1995)
- 14,400 (14.4K) models are between £75 and £100
- 28.8K bps models are about £200 and dropping in price

Data Compression and Error Correction

These two features go hand in hand and are complex subjects - beyond the scope of this text. Data compression is a system which compresses data to a ¼ or ½ its length or size for efficient and faster transmission. It has to be de-compressed at the other end. Error correction filters out line noise which could otherwise cause odd characters or garbled text to appear in the middle of words, making the text unreadable.

BABT Approval

You can buy American, British, German, French and Taiwanese manufactured modems. However, to connect a modem to the UK public telephone system, it must be approved by BABT. It is not illegal to buy and own an unapproved modem but under the Telecommunications Act you may be liable for prosecution if you use it.

CCITT and BABT

These are two 'names' you will come across. In Europe, the Committee Consultatif International Téléphonique et Télégraphic (CCITT - part of the United Nations) exists to provide for the standardisation of mobile and cellular radio-links and of data transfer methods and speeds. If your modem conforms to CCITT standards[27] then it should work correctly with other CCITT modems. However, the market abounds with cheap 'cloned' products, some of which have been known to fail to connect at higher speeds or to suddenly stop when in the process of transferring large files. Be careful then about buying a 'bargain' from a mail order catalogue.

An approved modem means, in our case, approved for use in the UK. The body responsible for such approval

---

[27] The USA does not conform to CCITT standards but this is changing rapidly. However, most USA modems recognise all relevant CCITT implementations.

is the British Approvals Board for Telecommunications (BABT). Approved modems of 1200 bps or less carry a Green Dot sticker. All modems of higher speeds do not have to carry a Green Dot sticker. However, all devices without BABT approval must carry a red triangle warning.

Only BABT approved modems are allowed to be connected to the PSTN (Public Switched Telephone Network) - not just British Telecom but any PPT (Post Telephone and Telegraph) supplier such as Mercury and cellular & CT2 networks. The BABT approval adds little to the overall cost of a modem but it does mean that it is safe for connection. However, it does not necessarily mean that the modem is "fit for purpose" (the relevant phrase in the Trades Description Act). In other words it may still not work correctly, in which case you must return it to the dealer, with all the hassle that entails. If you buy an unapproved modem, you may have a much more difficult time getting your money back or a replacement and you would get very little sympathy from the PPT supplier to which you tried to connect.

Choosing a suitable modem is not a simple task and we have mentioned only a few of the problems it entails. Although it may cost a few pounds more, it is safer to buy an approved modem from a reputable dealer who is also willing to help if things go wrong. Even better, choose an Internet Provider who, as part of the service, will supply one and advise you of the type you need. It is then their responsibility to ensure that you get connected properly.

Types of Modems

The type of modem you actually choose depends on whether you have a portable (laptop) or an office-type computer which sits on a desk. The latter usually requires a stand alone modem. It is a separate box with its own power supply lead, a second lead to plug into the telephone socket and a third into an RS232 socket. These are relatively small, consume little power but have a useful display panel which tells you what is going on.

If you have a portable computer, then you have a choice of a *card modem* which is simply plugged straight into your computer. These are usually cheaper but they do not have the advantage of a display panel. Otherwise you can opt for a *portable modem* which is about the size of a packet of cigarettes. These are battery powered and, of course, can fade just at the wrong moment. They are still relatively expensive.

Communications Software

Communication software is required to create a communication link between your PC, the modem and the computer which is connecting you to the Internet. There are several different kinds of software available from the basic to the more advanced. With the very basic level, you need experience in the use of *gopher* and/or *ftp* and possibly yet another communications program such as Kermit or PROCOMM.

Today, most Internet Service Providers use the more advanced software which conforms to one of two protocols - SLIP (Serial Line Internet Protocol) or PPP (Point-to-Point Protocol). Although these are different, each performs the same functions and brings the full power of the WWW browsers to your own doorstep.

Both require at least a 9600 bps modem. Your Internet Service Provider will tell you which protocol to use, since both your own communications software and that of the Service Provider must be compatible.

Choosing an Internet Service Provider

There are many different types of network systems connected to the Internet - university systems, commercial, academic/research and public/private systems. You could link your home computer to any one of these and make full use of the Internet. However, to do so, you would first need permission and, in most cases pay a fee for an account on their system. Each time you attempt to link to the Internet via their service network you will be required to give your account number (which is usually a name) to authorise your use. But which system to choose?

Unless you have some contact with a university or research organisation, you will choose one of the national commercial Internet Providers, such as EUnet, PING, Demon, SURFNET, etc. There are many more but all will offer telephone access (as well as direct leased lines for those who can afford it) to their large Internet connected computer systems.

Access is normally through a phone call to their nearest system, sometimes called Points of Presence (PoPs). Many of these companies are expanding all the time, establishing PoPs in many cities throughout the UK. Should one of these be local to your home, you will pay only for a local charge no matter where you connect to on the Net.

Choosing an Internet Provider means 'shopping around'. Choose one which provides a modem, helps to connect it and advises you on what communications software to buy so that you reduce many of the 'teething' problems you would otherwise have to face by yourself.

Commercial Internet Providers vary in what they offer and what they charge. Most will offer:

- direct connection to the Internet
- USENET news (now known as Network News)
- World Wide Web
- e-mail with multiple mailboxes for company organisations, most home users would require only one mailbox
- leased lines, again for commercial firms requiring direct, fast communication links by which they can send information to their world wide branches
- a choice of either SLIP or PPP communications protocols
- modem speed rates from 2400 to 28,800 bps
- a unique IP address
- installation configuration
- training
- consultancy and programming services

If I were to use the Demon company, my IP address could be: `j.shelley@thedrive.demon.co.uk`

where:

`j.shelley` is my name, I would choose this

`@thedrive` my street (or company) name, again I choose this, usually between 4 and 8 characters long[28]

---

[28] This can be extended but will depend upon what services the Internet Provider offers.

`demon.co.uk` - I cannot choose this since it is the domain name of the Demon company

Anything sent to me at that address, will be routed to the Demon's network storage system and stay there until I connect my computer to their system. My mail, or whatever, would then be forwarded to my own computer.

What Do the Providers Charge?

Clearly, this will vary. But one example is £12.50 for an initial registration fee and £10 a month after that. I would, of course, have to pay the normal charges to my existing telephone service provider such as BT, Mercury, Energis, etc., whilst connected to the Provider. Home users can normally pay on a monthly basis but company organisations often have to pay a full year's fee in advance and would be sent a formal VAT invoice. The usual procedure is to contact one of the Providers, discuss your requirements and they will advise you on what sort of package is most suitable, both hardware and software, and what their charges are.

The Overall Cost

A basic micro as outlined above (and at the time of writing) is about £800; a Pentium model is about £1200; a Pentium multimedia system, about £1500+. VAT is not included. A printer would be an optional extra of between £200 and £500+ depending on your requirements. In addition, the modem will cost between £40 and £200.

You will need Windows to run a WWW browser on a PC. Some browsers are free, others are free to charities and educational organisations.

Then there is the added cost if a service provider is involved. This can be as little as a standard registration fee, say £12.50 and a monthly rental of about £10 (plus VAT). Plus, your telephone bills.

Modem Standards

Modems which conform to the CCITT standards begin with a 'V', There are other 'standards' such as MNP. However, since the modem scene is changing all the time, consult your local modem dealer or Service Provider for current information.

The following lists some of the common V modems:

Standard	Speed	Time for 100K file Transfer
V.22	1200 bps	14 minutes
V.22bis	2400 bps	7 minutes
V.32	9600 bps	2 minutes
V.32bis	14.400 bps	85 seconds
V.34	28,800 bps	30 seconds
Standard		Service
V.42		Error Correction
V.42bis		Data Compression

Table 8

A good modem then would be a V.32bis with V.42 and V.42bis. Currently, such a model would range between £150 and £250. 100K is the average size of a file, either text or an image, sent over the Internet.

Chapter 11. Security: Hackers and Viruses

Can someone break into my machine and steal my data? Can people read my e-mail messages? Can my machine pick up a virus? Are my credit card details safe when I go shopping on the Internet?

When the Internet was used mainly for research by government and educational organisations, these issues were not major concerns. With commercial and private incursions into the Net, these issues have had to be addressed seriously. Just because you are on the Net, it does not mean that others can automatically break into your computer and steal your data or send you viruses, provided you take certain precautions.

Are my jewels safe in a bank vault? That depends on how security conscious the bank is. Likewise, once your machine is connected to the outside world via a local network, it is as secure as the network itself or indeed as secure as the communications software you use. One major software company is actually offering cash prizes to people who find flaws in its software after it was discovered that defects in the software allowed hackers to break into computer files.

Networks can be made very secure simply by restricting those who are allowed access. However, the whole purpose of the Internet is to allow anyone, anywhere to access information or any resource which a site is willing to provide. Consequently, the network which provides you with an Internet connection cannot be too restrictive.

Any computer, then, is potentially at risk. So precautions have to be taken. We shall look at large networks in general and then see what we can do to protect our own machine either at the office or at home.

Large Networks

Educational networks with valuable research information stored in their systems, or companies providing commercial services need to take certain precautions, especially on behalf of those customers paying for goods by credit cards. First the information or 'goods' have to be protected from direct and unauthorised theft. Secondly, customers' credit card details need protection.

With shopping on the Internet destined to become a multi-billion dollar marketplace, secure system software is being developed and tested. This we have to leave to the experts and trust that they can indeed create systems which will be safe. Two solutions are the use of *firewalls* and *encryption techniques*. The former are complicated systems and not easy to install except by professional companies. Firewalls attempt to stop or make it difficult for intruders to break into a system. In due course, firewall equipment may become common enough to drop in price and to be easily installed by anyone connecting to the Internet.

Another method is the use of encryption techniques. Information being carried over networks can be tapped into, just like telephone lines. Or the information could be left lying around on some other network. This could be an e-mail message which you have sent. One answer is to use an encryption program which scrambles the information before being sent over the network. When it reaches the other end, it needs to be de-crypted in order to be read.

Hackers or Crackers?

The term *'hacker'* in computing was originally almost one of respect. It referred to someone who was expert at a particular job, usually programming. In time, it was ascribed to those who were expert enough to break into computer networks. The early hackers were not malicious, it was enough just to break in and leave some evidence (called a *footprint*) of having done so, perhaps a message or access during non-operating hours.

Today's hackers are not from the old school, they frequently want to cause some damage to the system, to files, to databases, etc. They have broken into a whole range of systems from local credit companies to secret defence systems, and are now often referred to as *crackers*. Unfortunately, they are sometimes glorified by the media as heroes.

What is not so simple is the security of individual networks. The level of security depends on the conscientiousness and expertise of the local network administrators. The security of any network is down to passwords and network configuration. When a system is first purchased it is pre-set to factory defaults which, clearly, should be changed the moment the system is installed. Yet, it is not unusual for some networks not to do so. Anyone else with the same system will also know the factory settings.

It is probably better to assume that our network connection has a few holes somewhere through which hackers can slip through. Once into the network they can violate our computers. So is there anything we can do? Yes! We can take precautions and adopt certain ways of checking to see whether our micro is being violated.

Securing your Computer

When you connect (*log on* to) the network, you are asked for two pieces of information. First, an identification name so that the network can identify your machine as one of its valid users; what privileges have been granted to you; which files you have been allowed access to; and finally, which files belong to you. You cannot do anything about this user identification. Indeed, you may have to make it public, for example, if you wish to receive e-mail.

CERT

For large companies, discussing their security measures can be a problem, especially if their system has been broken into. Imagine a large firm of solicitors reporting publicly that their network was broken into and that the files of their clients held on disc had been copied or 'edited'!

The American government has funded an organisation called the Computer Emergency Response Team (CERT). Its aim is to investigate security problems, solve them and to provide other organisations with their solutions. Although their primary purpose is to deal with security personnel at company sites, they are able to respond to and help other individuals. Their e-mail address, at the time of writing, is:

```
cert@cert.org
```

The second piece of information is your *password*. A soldier's uniform is like your computer identity name. The uniform identifies him/her as having potential access to the barracks. However, to get past the guards and into the barracks a password has also to be given.

Computer passwords

Now this is something over which you have complete control. You invent a password and when used · it allows access to your office/home computer, and/or to the network to which your machine is connected. If you think of it as a pin number, then you will appreciate how careful you need to be. Anyone with your Access card and your pin number can use the card to extract money or go on a spending spree on your behalf.

It is in the creation of a secure password that you can make your machine safe. 80% of break-ins are due to weak passwords.

Creating Passwords

Passwords are normally up to eight characters in length taken from the following set:

- letters of the alphabet, where case is significant; thus `cat`, `CAT` and `cAt` are three totally different password names
- digits 0-9
- special characters, i.e. anything else on the keyboard which is not a letter or a digit

How do we invent a password? Perhaps we should first discuss what *not* to use as a password.

Never use your name, those of your children or grandchildren, vehicle number, insurance number, pet names, your house or street names, girl/boy friends name, anniversary dates. Programs exist which can try all these since they are public knowledge. Yes, the hackers will have to find out, but that is part of their 'trade'. They have to type them in, but the program will try using them as passwords even in reverse order and all combinations of upper and lower case.

Never use all numbers, it would not take a computer that long to exhaust all numbers between 00000000 and 99999999.

Never use common dictionary words. Hackers have programs which use all the words in a dictionary to see whether you have chosen one for your password.

So what password can you use and one which is easy to remember? One suggestion is to use a favourite phrase of your own such as: '*He wear's Cor Blimey Trousers*' (I am not implying its your favourite!). Use the first letters: HWcbT - using a mixture of case. Throw in the odd special character and a digit or two: HWcbT*78 - that is a perfectly good example of a password. Do not try using the name of your favourite TV programme, that is too easy.

Do not write the password down, but if you have to then never leave it in the drawer by your computer. Do not give it to someone else, but if you have to then change it as soon as the other person no longer has need of it.

Whether you give it to others or not, you ought to change the password every so often. How do you change your password? That will depend on the system you are using, therefore your first request from the network you are using is 'How do I change my password?' If they are really security conscious, this ought to be one of the first things *they* tell you before you have to ask them.

Should you ever forget your password, the systems administrator will be able to provide you with a new one. He/she will not be able to tell you your old one because when a password is entered into the system, it is encrypted before being stored in the password file. The encryption method is not reversible.

You can often tell whether your system has been broken into.

- When you log on to a system, some of them will tell you when you last logged on. You should get into the habit of checking this information. Should you be surprised to find that 'you' logged on at 2.30 am on Sunday morning when you know that you were fast asleep, then report it to your network administrator and change your password immediately.
- You may feel that your machine is slower than normal. This could mean that a virus is at work.
- You may become suspicious about some of your files. They may no longer be there or their size (number of bytes) has increased indicating the possible presence of a virus.

If you adopt these basic precautions about passwords, then you will reduce the risk of your machine being hacked into. By being more alert about your files and how your computer 'feels' then in the event of a break-in you can at least minimise the potential damage.

Viruses

Unfortunately, viruses can be picked up quite easily. If you load a program which has a virus onto you machine, you run the risk that the virus will infect it. The program could come from someone else's disc or, indeed, from the Net.

What can we do?

- be wary about public domain and shareware software. Try to use official sources rather than free, public software. By *official* I mean software developed by and accessed via reputable commercial companies
- before using new software, do a back up (make copies) of all your important files. Should your machine then get a virus which destroys your files, you have your original copies to fall back on
- buy the best anti-virus program available and install it on your computer. These programs, sometimes known as *vaccines*, will check your hard disc and memory each time your computer is switched on. They also check any floppy disc that you insert. If a virus is found, it is destroyed at source and before it can do any harm. However, you will need to keep the vaccine programs up to date since new viruses are appearing all the time
- keep reading the CERT Co-ordination Centre's news (see Appendix A for details)

Most virus problems have solutions and advice is available on the Internet via the CERT Co-ordination Centre based at Carnegie-Mellon University. If you suspect the possibility of a virus, contact your systems manager immediately. Yes, we all have 'scares' and think a virus is at work when it is something silly we have done. However, systems managers have a vested interest in keeping their systems clean. It is better to be safe than sorry.

It used to be thought that data files were immune from viral infections. That is no longer true. A new strain has emerged, called the *WinWord.Concept* virus (also known as WW6Macro and Prank Macro), which infects Word 6 documents. It can even be spread via e-mail. It makes use of the WinWord macro language, Word Basic, to infect Word documents. Each time a user saves a document, it becomes infected with the virus. Anyone else using that document will also be given the virus which will spread to any documents they save, and so on. Initially the virus was benign, but there are now reports that it is has become harmful.

Credit Card Details

One large retailer, offering shopping and a secure credit card system, found that its system had been broken into. Admittedly, it took 128 computers and two weeks effort to do so, but it was broken.

Virus

A computer virus is a program, deliberately written by a human being to cause an effect. These effects vary from harmless 'fun' such as a funny face or a rude message appearing on your screen to downright wanton destruction of networks, files, even hardware itself, for example the read/write arm of a disc drive. It is almost impossible to locate the perpetrator.

Computer viruses, like their biological counterpart, can spread from one machine to another. Some may delete user files, others may act like a cancer by destroying small parts of a database on a daily basis. Yet others may lie dormant until something activates them. This could occur by the virus checking the computer system's date. On a given date, it comes to life and wreaks havoc.

Viruses are picked up in a variety of ways. Another person's floppy disc may have a virus. If you use that disc, the virus may hop into your machine's hard disc and begin to infect your own floppy discs. Anyone else using their discs on your machine may now pick up the same virus and, infect their own machines. Colleges with computer rooms which are open to all students have to be particularly vigilant in guarding against this type of infection.

Loading public software over any network may result in your machine being infected with a virus hidden in the software. Networks themselves can pick up a virus and spread it around to other networks and to the user communities of those networks.

Chapter 12: Legal, Political and Moral Issues

The WWW provides a means for accessing information stored in various sites on the Internet. If I do get hold of some free software from some public domain and use it, could I be prosecuted? If I obtain permission via e-mail from an author to use his or her material, would it stand up in a court of law? As a distributor of information, am I liable for what someone else can post on my network? Could a college be prosecuted for what one of its students or staff disseminate via its network?

The law is not yet clear about such issues. Indeed, laws governing information technology in general are few. Those which do are open to different interpretations. This is where the EFF can help. Certainly, test cases will be needed to clarify points of law. To give an example, in June, 1995, a judge of the State Supreme Court in Mineola, New York, ruled that a certain information provider was a *publisher* rather than a simple *distributor* of information. This distinction meant that it could be sued for libel over some material which was posted to its financial electronic bulletin board by an unknown user.

The judge drew the fine distinction because the company uses humans and computerised systems to filter out objectionable material posted to its network. Not all information providers do this and, therefore, act along the lines of a book shop or library which simply distributes information. However, because this company screened messages, it was deemed to be acting as a publisher of information.

As a general user of the Internet, it is wise to be aware of some of these problems. For example, any e-mail message or contribution to a newsgroup sent from your machine will be attributed to you, even if it were sent by somebody else using your computer. You will be the one to bear the responsibility of any libel suit.

E-mail can remain on your system and come back to haunt you. You can delete it from your hard disc (which you should do regularly). However, it may still reside on the network. "But they ought to delete out-dated files from their discs every so often!", you cry! So they should, but how many odds and ends have you got lying around unused and unwanted on your hard disc? We often wait until some extra space is required, before doing this chore. So do system network people. Their discs are so vast, in terms of gigabytes[29], that some networks will not bother to delete files until some threshold is reached or extra space is required.

This means that some snoopy employers can rummage around employees mail messages on the network, despite the fact that you have deleted your rude messages about your boss from your hard disc. Again, what legal action may employers take against employees who 'abuse' the company e-mail service? Test cases are required to find out. The moral is that *you* should be careful.

Just who is legally responsible for what is allowed on the Internet is a complex issue since there is no one body responsible for controlling what goes on to the Net. It is the responsibility of each separate network in the overall web of networks. Bearing in mind that these networks are owned by government, commercial,

----

[29] giga = a thousand million, 10^9.

educational, private agencies, etc., and that they exist in over 69 countries each with its own laws, politics and customs, you can begin to see why it is so complex.

One university computer centre has had to apply guidelines, over 30 of them, for college users who put information onto the Net via the university network. Essentially, the college wishes to disassociate itself from any legal repercussions which could result from the material. Rightly so. Individual staff (or their heads of departments) have to sign a document making them responsible for any legal comeback. This also has a direct bearing on the conditions of employment. It certainly makes one think twice about what one puts up on the Web.

Legal Implications

Broadly speaking, there are at least three areas which affect what material goes on the Net:

- government subsidies, at least in some countries, pay for large sections of the Internet
- since the Internet is truly world wide, information will travel across national boundaries each with its own export laws
- when software is being carried from one place to another, intellectual rights and licence issues are raised

Subsidies

Whoever pays for a particular network has the right to say what that network will be used for. Therefore, I should not use my company's office computer to advertise my own personal business. If I have any doubt, then I should contact the network administrator and clarify the issue.

One simple case may help. A commercial company wanted to use a university teaching room which had micros linked to the Internet. The company, of course, would make a profit out of the courses to be offered, so would the university involved. The issue was that the network being used directly out of the university was an educational network which was not permitted to make commercial gains. It use was restricted to research and education. Yes, there are gray areas, but the main point was that the particular university was not permitted to hand over its resources to a commercial organisation. Now if university staff were giving the courses and making a profit for the college, that would have been a different matter.

When a site arranges for its Internet connection, it has to state whether the connection is to be used for commercial or educational purposes. If it is for educational use, then information tends to be routed over educational networks, such as SUPERJANET. If its use is commercial, then the information is routed over private networks.

Export Laws

Exporting anything, even software, requires a licence. Some things are not covered or restricted, some things are. Networking code and encryption code may well be restricted. In other words, being helpful to a colleague in another country by sending some program code may well be illegal.

Likewise, if the export of a supercomputer is not allowed by a certain country, then remote access from an outside country to that computer may be prohibited too. Network administrators have to be careful about who can be granted access rights to hardware at their sites. Could they be legally held responsible? That may have to be decided by the courts.

Property Rights

Copyright and patent laws vary from country to country. It may well be legal to allow a program to be copied within one country but a breach of law if it is sent outside. What can you do? If you give anything away on the Internet, find out to whom it belongs and get their permission. Be warned, it is not clear whether getting permission via an e-mail message may actually count as valid in a court of law.

Some software can be accessed via the Internet from public sources, for instance, operating system updates. These may be supplied free by the vendors but may well require a license from the vendor if it is to be *used*. You could find yourself with a problem if you were to take and use this public information without obtaining a licence. Obtaining the software may well be legal, but using it may not.

Politics

Since many of the networks in the Internet are funded by governments, educational bodies, commercial companies, etc., politics may well play a role in supporting ongoing funding. At present the Internet is seen as well worth supporting, but some with influence may not see it in the same light. They might argue that the money could be better spent on something else.

Imagine trying to propose and justify a budget for secondary school use of the Internet when pornography is so easily accessible! Not everyone would agree that the benefits of the Information Superhighway would outweigh its potential dangers.

Morals

Porn, theft of information and of credit card details, breaking into computers (homes) reminds us of our unhappy society. They all exist on the Internet too, but the difference is the scale. It is not for me to change society, it is for all of us to change it.

Some do use the Internet for their own evil purposes, do not be surprised. If it becomes too bad, will it mean the end of the Internet? Probably not, there are now too many networks, some could be closed, but there would still be many left. After all, that was the whole concept behind the Internet, to keep going even when some networks were destroyed. Perhaps we shall soon have an Internet police force, patrolling the Internet for corruption and crime.

Chapter 13: The Future and Conclusions

The National Science Foundation's network (NSFNET), one of the most important backbones of all the networks which originally formed the Internet, no longer exists. This is mainly due to the existence of the many commercial networks which now effectively make it redundant. NSF, as an organisation, still lives on but its network was reported to have been turned off on either 30th April or 8th May, 1995 according to which source you read.

Where is the Net Going?

Perhaps nowhere at all! With so many new people joining it everyday, it could soon become clogged up with the sheer volume of traffic (passage of information) congesting the existing network cables. In 1994, some 30,000 networks comprised the Internet, by 1995 the number had reached 100,000 and it is still growing.

Extra and faster network lines will have to be installed to cope with the growing volume of traffic. One way this expansion could happen is by an increase in the commercialisation of the Net. This will be mourned by the old Net hands who relished the academic and the well behaved manner of the early days.

It more than likely that to cover the cost of the extra lines additional fees will be charged. This is already happening even with some publicly funded networks. For example, fees are now being charged by the federally funded NSF & InterNIC Registration Services division which maintains domain names. Fees are now

$50 (US) per year. Academic institutions are also destined to make some form of contribution.

It will probably be the Service Providers who will bear the main brunt of this cost, and rightly so, since they are the ones who have accelerated the demand for the Internet use.

Yet, as one freelance feature writer for the Internet points out this is something to be applauded. It was argued that this independent source of funding for the InterNIC made it independent of any political interests. Furthermore, 30% of the income will be put into a legal fund to deal with potential lawsuits. Currently, it is the US taxpayer who would have to pay for any legal fees resulting from lawsuits over domain names. It has not been necessary so far.

Will the Internet Change?

At the time of writing, the Internet is still very much of a free spirit. There is still no real control over what is put onto the Net apart from whatever monitoring is performed by the local site's systems manager. Unscrupulous information providers are already corrupting the original ethos of the Internet, with their pornography, drug 'advice' and the like. There is also minimal information security.

All these issues will have to be addressed sooner or later, perhaps through some form of control by government laws. Whatever measures are taken it will change the way users access the Information Superhighway and, possibly, change its spirit.

Technology

From a technological viewpoint, the future looks exciting with the Net capable of taking over some of the functions previously the sole domain of the media and the telephone system. For example, at present we have to wait to hear news and weather broadcasts as and when TV stations put out such programmes. In the future, this could be taken over by the Net with users 'tuning in' when *they* want to.

With current technology being so expensive, we cannot all make use of the instant conference features whereby people in different continents can link together to see and hear each other live. Expensive direct, leased lines are required apart from the multimedia equipment. But it may not be too long before commercial centres are established and, for a fee, a family in the UK could link up live to another centre in Canada or Australia or wherever and enjoy a live 'gathering' with other members of the family. How long before such a system can be brought down in price so that each home could have one? Probably later rather than sooner, but there are already signs around that companies are exploring this possibility.

There is talk of a device which when linked to our TV set can create 3-dimensional images. Couple this with virtual reality technology and we can see the arrival of a new leisure and educational industry. The special hardware required to use virtual reality, such as the headgear and touch 'gloves', is expensive, but may not remain so for too long. With the developments in super-density Roms (SD-Roms) and the growth of the Internet, it could be possible to pick-up movies from one site and run them on our own TV sets. They would be in 3-D and we could 'walk into' the film itself and touch objects as though we were actually in the film.

There are obvious implications here for education, the disabled and shopping, as discussed below.

Education

Some aspects of education could be revolutionised too. Text books are fine, they have pictures and diagrams as well as text. But imagine if one could click on a picture and the whole thing becomes animated with sounds to boot! This is already possible with some CD-Rom encyclopaedias. Couple this with *virtual reality* technology with different sites world wide preparing the material for the Internet and it could be made available to all parts of the world.

There may no longer be a need to make a day trip to the Science Museum in London. The school outing may well consist of switching into the Net and by means of virtual reality, the children could 'visit' the museum as though they were physically there. This concept, of course, is of value to the disabled not only for visits to a museum but to their 'local' supermarket.

It may not be too long before we can sit in front of our TV and go shopping to our 'local' supermarket. We could walk through the aisles, touch the goods on sale, order the items and have them delivered to our front door. Whether this is good for society is debatable. Someone was quoted as saying that it will be the delivery man's job that people will want since he/she will soon be the only one to meet people.

Shopping

Already a limited number of companies sell their products over the Net. One recent example, cited in a daily national newspaper, is that of an established cake-maker in the North of England. They have been using traditional recipes for over 100 years but their marketing techniques are the latest. The managing director explained that increasing sales for a small family firm in a fairly remote part of England was difficult. But now new orders are coming in from all over the UK, Europe and even the States.

The advertising costs on the Internet were cheap compared to traditional costs. The firm paid the service provider a small initial fee to set up the pages and now pays £60 a year 'ground rent' plus £100 fee to keep them live on the system.

How soon before many more find it necessary and beneficial to sell their products over the Net? Insurance, accountants, solicitors, finance companies, etc., could find new business, perhaps even world-wide.

Conclusions

The Information Superhighway and the Internet have grabbed the media's attention. Most books and articles on the Internet which I have read seem to imply that we cannot wait to get connected. Is this really true for all of us?

I have been most impressed by the rich source of information which is already available on the Net. But I must confess that I rarely use it. It takes too long for the information to appear on my screen and quite frankly there are too many other things to do. Much of the information I want can be accessed from alternative sources. Is there too much information? One cynical journalist thinks that we shall learn less and less about more and more. Perhaps he is right!

For many, myself included, it is expensive to set up an Internet connection from home. If that is so, is it not even more so for the Third World (*Developing Countries* - I think is the politically correct term). How are they to benefit from this Information Superhighway? I am sure they will in time, especially from the potential in education.

Personally, I wonder about a society in which individuals lock themselves into their rooms surfing around the Net. Yes, you can join in discussions but it is just you and your computer screen or, perhaps worse, just you under your virtual reality headgear.

Like most technologies, the Internet is here to stay and has some great potential. But it is early days. The technology has a long way to go before all of us will need to use it. I suspect that it will be the educational and the leisure markets that will make it a tool which we will all go out and buy. Some 'black box' will link to our home TV and we will be able to see 'things' in 3-D, touch them, visit places of interest, learn new skills without the danger of being hurt, rather like pilots who currently train on aircraft simulators. But some would still prefer to climb the slope and to see and hear and smell Mount Vesuvius in person.

The Information Superhighway has much to offer. In time we shall all be enmeshed in its web. It is now an important tool for companies, institutions and so on for contacting colleagues world wide by e-mail, promoting their images, ordering goods. It is of value to academic and research institutions which need to find material relating to their work. It appeals to those who can use their company's Internet connection to rummage around places of cultural and artistic interest. It certainly satisfies the mainly American craze for taking part in discussion groups.

But for many of us, we may have to await developments. The digital renaissance, as one author has put it, has arrived. But it is early days yet. For the moment, if you do have access to the Internet at home, do not forget to switch off your modem at night. One colleague of mine forgot. Unfortunately, he was linked to the States!

Smilies

Turn the page sideways to make out these little faces. There are many, many more. See Appendix A for WWW reference.

:-o	Wow!
:-|	grim
:= |	baboon
:-[	pouting
:=#	my lips are sealed
`-)	wink
(-:	user is left handed
{:-)	user wears a toupee
*<:-)	user is wearing a Santa Claus hat
[:-)	user is wearing a Walkman
=:-)	smiley punk rocker
~~:-(	net flame
3:]	pet smiley
3:[	mean pet smiley
B:-)	sunglasses on head

Glossary:

account   consists of your user identification, password as well as whatever access rights have been granted to you. In order to gain access to a network, you need to register and be given an account.

address   either an e-mail address, so that messages can be sent directly to a person, or the site address of a network on the Internet.

anonymous ftp   permits users to retrieve files from an ftp site without the need for an account.

Archie   a system for finding files which are publicly available by anonymous ftp. Archie provides a list and the location of the ftp sites.

ASCII   American Standard Code for Information Interchange. A code for representing characters and which is supported by almost all computer manufacturers.

BABT   British Approvals Board for Telecommunications. Only BABT approved modems can be used legally in the UK.

backbone   Any large, fast network system which connects a variety of smaller networks. NSFNET was one of the original backbones of the Internet.

BBS   Bulletin Board System. Most are now commercial and allow more than just posting messages for others to read and respond to.

bps bits per second; the speed at which binary digits are transmitted over a communication medium, such as modems and networks.

bridge a device which connects incompatible networks so that data can be transferred between them; see also *gateway*.

browsers programs used to explore the World Wide Web, WWW, using hypertext.

CCITT the Committee Consultatif International Téléphonique et Télégraphic, it produces the technical standards for data communications. Now replaced by ITU-T.

Cello a WWW browser.

Cix Compulink Information eXchange, one of the largest conferencing systems in the UK.

client a program which extracts a service or information on your behalf from a server computer somewhere on a network.

conference part of a BBS set aside for messages relating to a defined subject area.

dial-up connecting to another computer via the telephone system.

DNS Domain Name System which translates domain names into the numeric numbers used by the Internet Protocol (IP).

domain name part of the address name of a host computer on the Internet.

dotted-quad quaint term for the four numerical numbers separated by dots and used by the Internet addressing system.

e-mail address	a unique address used to forward messages to a specific computer on a network.
EFF	Electronic Frontier Foundation, an American organisation which addresses social and legal issues arising on the Internet.
encryption	a method of encoding data so that it is difficult to read by those not authorised to read it.
ethernet	one type of high speed local area network.
FAQ	short for Frequently Asked Questions (rhymes with *back*). Users are encouraged to look through the list of answers before asking a question which may already have been answered.
file server	a computer which stores files on the Internet and makes them available to those with permission.
firewall	a security device to protect private networks from Internet hackers.
flame	an abusive attack against someone who has posted a newsgroup message to which someone violently objects. Flame wars erupt when others join in and keep repeatedly sending out their flames.
ftp	file transfer protocol - a standard method of transferring files between, often, distant sites.

gateway   a computer system which allows incompatible networks to transfer data, such as e-mail. One network will convert the data into a format which the other can accept.

gopher   a menu type system for browsing around the Internet.

home page   the default page you see each time you call up your WWW browser. You can choose to make your own home page or use someone else's. Each site creates its own home page.

host   a computer on a network which allows remote users to access its facilities.

HTML   HyperText Mark-up Language is the language used to create pages of information on the WWW.

http   the Hyper-Text Transfer Protocol is used extensively by WWW to transfer information between networks.

hyper-media   a combination of hypertext and multi-media.

hypertext   text or images which contain a link to where further information about the phrase or picture is stored. By clicking on a piece of hypertext, a new page of information pops up.

hypertext-link   the link address of where some more information is stored about some hypertext.

IAB   Internet Architecture Board, a group which makes decisions about Internet standards and other important matters.

IETF   Internet Engineering Task Force, a voluntary group which investigates technical problems and reports back to the IAB.

IP   Internet Protocol, the rules by which the many different computers on the Internet can communicate.

ISDN   Integrated Services Digital Network, a digital telephone service which allows high speed access to the Internet, if you have the appropriate hardware and software, and if your service provider supports it.

ISOC   Internet SOCiety, the main governing body of the Internet to which the IAB report.

ITU-T   International Telecommunications Union Telecommunications which replaced the CCITT.

LAN   Local Area Network, a collection of computers which can communicate with each other in a local vicinity such as a building.

leased line   a permanently connected and private telephone line linking two computers together, such as a local network to an Internet Provider. They start around £10K per annum, not for the average home user. But for many businesses with overseas interests, they can be remarkably cost effective.

line noise   interference on the telephone line which can distort computer communication.

listserv   an automated mailing list system which distributes e-mail

login   the process of typing in your user name and password to gain access to a network on which you have an account.

lurker   someone who reads discussion group mail but who does not wish to add to the conference/discussion.

mail reflector   a special mail address. Mail sent to this address is automatically forwarded to a discussion group's mailing list.

mailing list   a list of e-mail addresses, typically all those taking part in a particular discussion.

MIME   Multipurpose Internet Mail Extensions, a method of encoding files so that not only text but images, sound and videos can be sent via e-mail.

modem   MOdulator-DEModulator, a device which allows data to be transferred between computers via the telephone system.

multi-media   not just text but also images, sound, video

network administrator   each network has its own network systems administrator or manager. It is the role of this person to see to the smooth running of the network and to provide assistance to all users. In many cases, the manager is responsible for the security of the network and for monitoring what is allowed to be put up on the network for access by other users.

newsgroup   a message area or forum for Network News relating to a defined subject matter.

newsreader   a program which allows news to be read or posted.

OLR   Off Line Reader. A program which is used to access data on a bulletin board. It allows you to read and reply to messages off-line saving your telephone bills. Messages are sent directly to your hard disc and the telephone connection broken. You read and reply at your leisure.

outernets   all networks which are not part of the Internet.

packet   data transmitted over the Internet are broken into smaller packets, usually about 1500 characters. They have to be re-assembled at the other end.

post   to send a message to a conference or newsgroup.

PPP   Point to Point Protocol; communications software which allows a computer to use the Internet via the telephone.

protocol   standards or rules which define how information is passed between computers.

router   a computer which transfers data between two networks which use the same protocols.

server   software which allows one computer to offer a service to another computer. Client software on the other computer, requests the service from the server. Sometimes, the computer with the server software is also called the server.

service provider   an organisation, either academic or commercial, which allows other computers to access the Internet through its own network.

shareware   software which you can try out before you buy it. If you like it, you register with the producer and pay a fee.

site   any of the networks which comprise the Internet.

SLIP   Serial Line Internet Protocol, communications software which allows a computer to use the Internet via the telephone.

smiley   smiling faces consisting of ASCII characters used in e-mail and similar messages to denote joy or sadness. Turn the page sideways and see if you can make these out.   :-(:-) Some use a semi-colon to denote a wink   ;-)

subscribe   to join a discussion group by being added to its mailing list.

system manager   see network administrator

TCP   Transmission Control Protocol, the system which breaks up data into smaller *packets* for transmission over the Net.

telnet   a simple protocol which allows you to login to a remote network.

threads   a series of postings about a particular
                   discussion or conference. There is the initial
                   thread, which starts the whole discussion
                   going, and other threads which form part of
                   the subsequent discussion.

UDP   User Datagram Protocol, one of the many
                   protocols used over the Internet.

URL   Uniform (or Universal) Resource Locator.
                   The method of specifying the location of
                   resources on the Internet. Used mainly with
                   WWW.

USENET   USErs' NETwork. The group of systems
                   which exchange 'news'. Now more
                   commonly known as Network News.

Veronica   Very Easy Rodent-Oriented Netwide Index
                   to Computerised Archives - (I wonder how
                   long it took to invent that one?). It is built
                   into gopher to allow keyword searches at
                   gopher information sites.

virtual reality an artificial 3-dimensional world, which
                   combines computer images and special
                   hardware. Users can move around and
                   handle objects in this 'virtual world'.

WAIS   Wide Area Information Systems, a tool
                   used for searching databases stored on the
                   Internet.

WAN   Wide Area Network. A network which may
                   be national or global in extent, as opposed
                   to a local area network.

white pages   an electronic phone book or database which stores people's e-mail addresses and sometimes postal addresses, telephone number, etc. There are several different kinds of white pages servers some of which are accessible through the WWW.

workstation   a larger and more powerful type of computer than the simple micro. They are frequently the computers used in a LAN and based upon the Unix operating system.

WWW   short for World Wide Web

Appendix A

Here are a few places to visit on the Internet. We acknowledge the sites and URLs mentioned. However, URLs and sites come and go, what works today may not work by the time this book is published.

URLs would be typed in the Location Box as seen on page 66. If the address is not known, then the WWW browsers have a Net Search button which when clicked will allow you to type in a word or phrase in simple English and provide a list of sites which match your keywords. By using Net Search, you can begin to compile your own list of places to visit.

The British Library has a gopher site:
gopher://portico.bl.uk

The Science Museum, London - home page:
http://www.nmsi.ac.uk/

The Unofficial Smiley Dictionary:
http://www.tu-chemnitz.de/~lpo/smiley_dict.html
(I found this by using the Net Search for the word smiley.)

The UIUC Weather machine:
gopher://wx.atmos.uiuc.edu

CIA World Factbook, an immense resource:
gopher://gopher.uwo.ca

White House Papers:
http://sunsite.unc.edu

Doctor Fun, the Net's own daily cartoon:
http://sunsite.unc.edu/Dave/drfun.html

ElNet Galaxy: a huge WWW site which searches the Internet for any imaginable topic.
http://galaxy.einet.net/galaxy.html

USENET newsgroup descriptions and FAQs:
gopher://owl.nstn.ns.ca

USENET newsgroups, a good place for the beginner:
Type this in the Net Search box:
news.announce.newusers
try this as well: news.newusers.questions

ISOC: gopher://gopher.isoc.org
or e-mail: isoc@isoc.org

For information about viruses:
Type this in the Net Search box: comp.virus

CERT: e-mail address: cert@cert.org
To join the mailing list: cert-advisory-request@cert.org
or: cert-tools-request@cert.org

Where to find free and commercial databases:
http://ukoln.bath.ac.uk

Business resources can be found at the CityScape site: http://www.cityscape.co.uk

If you want to order cakes or to see how you can go shopping, try:
http://www.octacon.co.uk/bothams

INDEX

127

Please note: **f** after a page reference indicates following pages.